Healing

Other books by Rod Campbell:

Love, Kindness and Prayer can Perform Miracles

Memories of an Old New Zealand Horseman

At One with Nature

Healing from Love

Healing through Love, Kindness and Respect for All Living Things

Rod Campbell

Awareness Book Company

Auckland, New Zealand

Awareness Book Company Ltd.

P.O. Box 9224, Newmarket

Auckland, New Zealand

ISBN 0-9583558-2-7

Cover design by Rod Campbell

Illustrations by Rod Campbell

Printed in New Zealand by GP Print

Printed on Recycled Paper

Rod Cambell, Hikurangi, New Zealand

Acknowledgments

To all the families of the old people who taught me so much by their example in my early life. By the respect they had for others. For always having a kind word or a helping hand whenever it was needed. In those days most people barely had enough to survive on. But these families were willing to share what little they did have with any in need, whether it was a lost or wounded small animal or a dying person. There were so many, but to just mention a few. Some were very capable people in many ways and helped always with no thought of recognition or reward.

Mrs Amy Mills of Te Karaka, a widow with five children who was on call 24 hours per day if anything God created needed help.

My own parents whose home was always open to anyone in need. My Aunt Annie Smale who spent her life helping others. Also Annie's brother Dr Rex Smale.

Our first neighbours Billy and Puti Walker. The Wainui family. The families of Rubin Browns, Sam Robins, Tommy Smith, Jim Sinton, Jim Moores, Bill Bartlet, Pa Ruru, Ted, Bill and Frank Tait, Harry Hollis, Hughie Seymour, Rangi Puru, Sonny and Sedon Jones, Don Anderson, Bill Picken, Bill O'Mera and Ray Renata and Harry Redmond.

MY THANKS TO GOD for bringing me in contact with the people who have shared so much with me in helping others and then spent time and given a great deal of support in recording our experiences. There are far too many to thank but just to mention a few of the first who helped so much. Elizabeth Vanderham, Boz-enka Stefulic, Bonnie Lou Yoroshka, Caprice and Elizabeth Hogg, John Darragh, Nancy Dudley, Craig Riley, Debra Komar, Dr. Logan Stanfield, Dr. Logan Doubler, Dr. Norman Shealey, Dr. Bernie Seigal, Cassie Weiss Zellner, Edgar Wilson and many others in Alaska and in many parts of Canada and the USA.

Foreword

This book brings together the experiences in the life of Rod Campbell with particular emphasis on the influences on him in his formative years and his experience as a healer. The influences in his formative years included his closeness with the natural world and the people young and old he admired as he grew up. Of particular note was his empathy with animals including horses, dogs and birds. His experience as a healer has helped many people in Canada, the United States and New Zealand. Many of the healings were both amazing and durable. His simple uncomplicated approach of the pure expression of love, kindness, prayer and respect for all living things has made him especially effective in using his healing gift.

This book has extensive extracts from two of his previous books, *Memories of an Old New Zealand Horseman* and *Love Kindness and Prayer can Perform Miracles,* as well as new material to provide a complete overview of his earlier life on livestock farms and his later life as an instrument of healing energy. A few of the healing stories have been repeated with a variation in content in different sections because they are relevant to more than one theme in the book.

Rod's style of writing is as if he were having a conversation with you. The editing has been minimised with the aim of retaining as much as is possible this conversational style.

Ashton Wylie

Contents

Introduction

This book has been written hoping that other people can learn from my experiences and will be able to use my observations and stories to benefit them in their lives.

I wish to pass on the love and kindness I have received and also wish to help others do the same. I wish to help others to see the benefit of living with love and respect for all living things and to see that this is not just a matter of words—it is a way of life.

In this book I have drawn on material from my previous two books, "Memories of an Old New Zealand Horseman," and, "Love, Kindness and Prayer can Perform Miracles," together with new stories arising from experiences occurring since they were written.

Included in this book are letters from people who have received benefit from healing. They will be printed as they were written. These are included to show that love, respect and healing energy with prayers does work; not to show that the credit they give me is justified—it is no credit to me. This universal energy is all around us just waiting to be used to help each other, our planet and all living things.

My own feeling now is that it is not too late in my life to make a difference by conveying my experience of love and kindness through this book to help people to heal themselves and to heal others.

My guidance is to use this book to encourage others, particularly younger people, to realise the value of kindness, respect and prayers and to use kindness, respect and prayers to help others.

Although this book provides guidance and help for people who want to help others it must also be realised people can help others even if they themselves are very sick, not educated or cannot read or see very well.

The messages are simple and come from the heart:

Love, kindness and respect can be given freely without speaking one word. This is greatly appreciated and can change the lives of all living things.

All Living Things

There are a lot of people doing far more than I could ever do by directing this universal energy with love and kindness. All living things use this energy to help others. When a cat was run over on the road in Canada over a mile from the ranch house, a dog went away three times and brought back three kittens and put them in a box at the back door. How did this dog get that message or guidance?

A dog trainer had a big, very vicious dog that was making endless attempts to get off the chain to go into the yard close by. When finally the trainer let him out, he rushed to a tree where a little bird with no feathers had fallen out of the nest and he held it in his mouth. Thinking that was the end of the bird, the trainer left him alone for some time while wondering if that dog really was too vicious to be trained, as so many people said he was. Later he found the dog was just holding the bird in his mouth to keep it warm, just as we would have held it in our hand. Then the dog stood quietly by while the bird was put back in the nest in the tree. This dog was ready to start work searching for anything in distress and needing help, but how could he let people know?

There are thousands of stories of animals helping others of a different species and also thousands of stories of peoples' lives being saved by an animal, and animals even giving their lives to save someone.

All living things are one family

There are thousands of people and creatures of every sort who have done far more than I will ever be able to do, by being guided to use this loving healing energy. They allow this universal loving healing energy to flow through them to help others and help preserve life on our planet.

People of every nationality have told me how they were guided closer to God and nature through connections with a bird. There is no time or space to write all their stories at this stage, but the following is how a little girl's kindness towards a little bird changed my life and the lives of hundreds of people on the other side of the world. It was my daughter's kindness towards a little bird that was responsible for the knowledge that this energy was available and could be used, often with amazing results.

Love, kindness and prayers

(Auckland, New Zealand)

After almost 20 years of pain caused by being under a horse that turned end over end on top of me, the doctors decided to put me in the Lavington hospital in Auckland, New Zealand to have a bone graft. During the operation there was a power failure and undistilled water was blown back from a suction pump into the wound. This caused an infection in the wound which spread into the bone.

After 12 months the bone graft broke again and I was put into the Mater Hospital (now Mercy Hospital) for another operation. There I learnt the true meaning of kindness. The Sisters were all nuns and used to work 12 hours per day, seven days per week, for no pay. If you had been giving them five thousand dollars per day they couldn't have done more for you. Visitors from out of town were made most welcome and were always given a drink of tea, just as if they were part of a family.

In those days operations were done with chloroform, causing you to vomit all night. After a big operation you felt very sick, but all night there seemed to be someone sitting beside your bed to wipe your face or help in any way. The kindness you received there from the staff was something you couldn't buy with money.

The treatment wasn't hard to put up with for the six week stay there. When this bone graft also broke again, it was necessary to come back to have it done once more. There were many more tests and X-rays done. Then I was told the infection in the bone wouldn't improve and that it would only get worse. They would do one more bone graft and put in a steel bar, but I was never to think of working again or doing anything because it was only going to get worse and that I would be in a wheelchair before too long.

The thought of going into a wheelchair didn't frighten me because I had seen a man riding in a horse show who had been a lesson to me. After the show I had mentioned something about his riding and someone said, "Don't you know who that is? He is Geoff, our Member of Parliament. He has one leg, one arm and one eye." There was something about him that made you know nothing would stop him from doing what he thought he needed to do. The thought of what he had gone through and could still do gave me great hope.

When Geoff was wounded in the desert they cut his arm off without anaesthetic before shifting him out. Then they decided not to take his leg off because he was going to die anyway. While waiting to die, he was very uncomfortable because they were putting maggots in his leg to eat up all the poison. But unknown to the doctors he used to get someone to bring a leaf off a tree near the hospital and lay it on his leg. While the leaf was withering it would draw all the discomfort away from his leg, then he would get a fresh one and put it on his leg every two days. He visited me recently and at the age of 82 is still as capable of riding a horse over jumps or doing anything anyone else can do. When he was voted into Parliament in his forties two doctors who examined him said he might live to 50 but definitely wouldn't reach 60. He came to see me a few weeks ago. It is doubtful if those doctors who predicted his demise are alive today. I didn't know at the time, but the fact that I had seen Geoff ride in the show had put me in the right frame of mind to be able to overcome anything.

I was prepared to leave everything to God, and enjoy every moment and forget all about the past or any worries or stress and appreciate every moment while I was here. With the experience I have had since then, I know the people with that attitude can overcome anything—no matter what it is.

I had this attitude but didn't even know it. Neither did the man who was responsible for my complete recovery.

Painting and drawing was one thing I always loved doing and used to do in hospital for the nurses and staff. In fact when the doctors came in to see me they always seemed more interested in what I had drawn than in my condition. So I was looking forward to my wheelchair and knew that as long as I had one eye and one hand I could paint. What encouraged me was that people seemed to like what I drew and painted.

Three weeks after the X-ray I was opened up for the final operation. A doctor came to see me afterwards and said there is no way it could be explained, but when they opened up my back the bone that had been all broken three weeks earlier was sound and they could not find any sign of the infection that had been there all that time.

I worked hard on the farm for over 40 years after that, doing all the things that should be hard on a person's back, and never had one bit of pain. I did ache in every joint and muscle from the hard work, but never did have any pain in the spine.

The nuns and others were praying for me before the operation and I didn't even know until months later. I haven't had any time to sit still and paint ever since, but in that hospital I did learn the value of love, kindness and prayers. I am very privileged to be doing what I do now, which is passing on the love, kindness and prayers I received in that hospital. I will always be grateful to God for letting me have that experience, and for allowing me to feel those years of continual pain before the operation and the love and kindness which allowed me to recover.

A *change of attitude*

(Pakotai, New Zealand)

The people who have permanent recoveries, even after being told there was nothing medical science could do for them, are the people who have a complete change of attitude. After being told they have a very short time to live, they then see and appreciate the little things they never had time to see before. They now appreciate the little things they hadn't even thought of previously.

My own experience of the effects of a change in attitude was a lesson to me. I had been crushed by a tree and while in hospital had developed a blood clot in one leg. After leaving hospital it was necessary for me to return every two days for a blood test. After travelling one hour home, they would phone to tell me what coloured tablets to take to keep my blood condition right.

This day I was feeling terrible and was down milking the cows before going to hospital. It had been raining for weeks and everything was wet, coats and boots never dried properly and there was mud everywhere. The cow bail was leaking and there was a cold wind blowing. I was thinking to myself, what a terrible place this was for an old man of my age to be living. The mist was right down on the hills and water was dripping from all the trees and everything. I wondered what I had done to deserve living under these conditions.

After going to hospital and having the blood test the farm where I lived and worked seemed even worse on return. Because I didn't feel very good, I just wanted to lay down, but there was a message from the hospital to come straight back in; to make sure to get there as quickly as possible and not to let anything stop me from getting there. There were doubts in my mind as to whether I was going to reach the hospital or not. Then as time went on these doubts became stronger and I had almost convinced myself that I wasn't going to get there. However, we did get there and after a few hours everything was in order again and I was able to return home and to encounter a very changed outlook to the environment of the farm.

The next morning it was still raining when I went out to milk the cows. I first breathed in some beautiful fresh air and thought how wonderful it was, then saw all the beautiful lights sparkling on every drop of water dripping off every leaf, flower and blade of grass. Then there were the lights and shadows shining in the mist and clouds rolling down over the hills. On walking through wet grass with sparkling little streams running everywhere, there were two fantails keeping me company as I was driving the cows to be milked. The air was so fresh and everything so bright and clean I thought this must be the cleanest and healthiest place for an old man to have the privilege to live, enjoy and appreciate nature and be part of it all. I did hope from then on I would be able to always appreciate the privilege of sharing it all with my family and all our animals. I also hoped we would always be able to appreciate being part of nature and be able to enjoy the best of every season and change in weather.

When my mental attitude had changed so much from just being bored and resentful of everything to loving and appreciating everything, it must have made a difference to how my body reacted because I felt much healthier. From that time on I never ceased to appreciate all the good things in nature. This also made me more aware of how many living things needed kindness and support.

In many cases where people have been told they only have a short time to live, they realise later they were very privileged people because it gave them a chance to change their lives completely. Then they were able to appreciate and enjoy every moment from then on.

The first healing—the little bird

(Pakotai, New Zealand)

At Pakotai in the far north of New Zealand, my seven year old girl chased a cat around the house dozens of times trying to rescue a little bird it was carrying. Finally with sweat and tears running down her face she brought what looked like a dead bird to me and said, "Dad, can you do anything to help this bird?" I said, "I can't, but God may be able to." So holding the bird gently in my hands I asked God in the name of Jesus Christ if he would let his healing power go through my hands to help the little bird's body to heal itself. Soon there was a warm glow in my hands and after checking the condition of the bird a few times by opening my hands we were able to see movement in its neck, where the pulse showed the heart was beating again.

I tried to hold up its head up for a few moments, but it would just drop down again when released. The warm glow around it seemed to become denser. Then as time went on, it was able to hold its head up on its own.

We then took it out on the big verandah in the warm sun, where there was a lot of soft grass down below so it wouldn't get hurt if it tried to fly, but we didn't even think it would try. There were tall blue gum trees above us and dead silence everywhere. It seemed as if there wasn't a bird for miles around.

After sitting in the sun for some time with the bird in my open hand I was able to see it was starting to look around. Then suddenly it flew out of my hand and before it had gone six feet there were over thirty birds there with it, flying around and around making a terrific noise, flying up to the top of the tree and back down to us, flying so close to us that they were almost touching us, all the time singing and rejoicing.

God's Messenger

No prayer of thanks could have been said more plainly than what those little birds were saying. We couldn't speak for a few moments, but felt a great presence of love and peace. I am sure God heard their prayers of thanks as they continued their singing and dancing for a long time. I was then guided to say, "That just shows what a little bit of kindness can do. It didn't cost us anything and didn't only help one but made a difference to all those birds. They must have been watching all the time from when the cat caught it until it flew back to them."

When your health is not good there are times when a little bit of kindness is worth more than all the money in the world.

Having seen hundreds of miracles since then, I know that with love, kindness and prayers anything is possible.

Calling to Canada

(Warkworth, New Zealand)

After the success with the little bird, there were many occasions where people would complain of aches and pains, and I would be urged to ask to let me see what I could feel from them. Without touching the person it was possible for me to feel the pain going through my left hand and feel it getting less until the person said it was gone.

From then on I had this urge to go to Canada. The week before leaving I had met a healer, Delores Winder from Texas, in a church at Warkworth. She had said to the Minister that the healing I had described to her which was given to the little bird had come from God and that I should be encouraged to join the Church and attend their bible classes. I explained that I was going to Canada and wouldn't be able to attend.

She asked why I was going and I said I had such a strong urge to go but didn't know why. She said, "When you get there you will meet the people you need to meet and the people who need you will find you." I explained that it would be nice to have one week's rest first and then find out why I was there. I only knew one person in Canada. The night I arrived three visitors from South Africa asked for healing, the next day there were eight more and the third day I was asked to a clinic where 15 more people asked for healing.

Of these, six were told beforehand that there was nothing medical science could do for them and they were sent home to die. After healing they all went into remission straight away so their doctors came to find out why. After that the doctors unofficially referred other patients to me or came for treatment themselves. One doctor had been around the world getting treatment for a leg with no circulation, without success. There was also a lump on his leg below the knee. The next day there was good circulation in his leg and the lump had gone. After that he sent many more patients.

This doctor had a patient whose kidneys weren't working, her pancreas wasn't working, she had had diabetes since she was 4 years old, was going blind in one eye and getting gangrenous in one foot. Her blood pressure was so high they couldn't give her a kidney transplant. She had only a short time to live. In six days her kidneys were working and her blood pressure was down to normal.

From then on I was kept busy seven days per week and had fares paid to go to many places all over Canada and the U.S.A. I carried on doing this work for six years. No doctor could send patients to me officially for fear of losing his licence, but their nurses could give them my phone number so they could get in touch with me if they wanted to. Letters and comments from patients, practitioners and others have been included in this book.

Planting the seed

(Calgary, Alberta)

In the quiet corner of the day, among people whose bodies are being destroyed and deformed by disease, guilt and fear, between healing and tears, I often think of a person who is very special to me. She was the first one to whom I was guided when I first arrived in Canada. Today I know it was no coincidence.

We met late one summer afternoon a few years ago. I was sitting on the stairs, just new to Canada, thinking about family and friends in New Zealand. I knew that I had to come. Suddenly I was overwhelmed by an urge to turn my head, and there was a woman in the neighbour's yard looking at me. A strange feeling swept over me and made me stand up. I started walking, the woman was walking, time stood still. I knew we had never met before, but in the blink of an eye we recognised each other and I understood that I had come home.

From that day on Boz-enka was like a mother to me. Through her I met many wonderful people, who helped me in so many different ways. Boz-enka had an ability to see things happen and they did happen. The very first day we met I was worried about how to find people that needed healing. "You don't look for people, they will come to you. I see hundreds of them coming," she said—and it happened. I started working around the clock.

Little Amy was dying from leukemia. There was no hope. Chemotherapy had failed, science was hopeless, drugs did not work, but love, kindness and prayer did. Day after day Amy came to me for healing treatment. Her parents had spent more than they could afford on specialists and other things. The mother asked how much the treatment would cost and how often she would have to come. When I told her that it was not going to cost one cent and that Amy should come every day until she was better, I knew that she was going to recover. It seemed that every day new stars were born in her eyes. When she next went to hospital for a check up in 11 days time, there was no sign of the disease.

I returned to visit Boz-enka to share my happiness. "A miracle has happened," I said. She looked at me blankly. "You don't understand," she said, "When a sick body gets well again, that is not a miracle." Healing is to be understood as a natural process.

As a young child Boz-enka was very close to her grandfather who was both a priest and a philosopher. He was a very gifted man. He died when she was eight years old. Two days before he died he called the little girl Boz-enka to his side and gave her many pages of handwriting he had done. "This is your inheritance," he said. "Don't lose it before you are able to understand it."

The little girl saved the writings through fire and flood, taking them across three different continents. On the way to Canada, they were her most precious possessions. They were her only inheritance. These writings proved to be about the things we are trying to do today: surrendering to love, kindness, honesty and prayer. The ability to heal body and soul is something that is given to us so generously. Physically there is only so much one person can do, but spiritually there are no limitations.

People came for help, hundreds of them—they are still coming. God's power coming through my hands seemed stronger, but since I was getting older, I couldn't rejoice at our successes, but only worry about all the ones needing help, especially children, whom we were unable to meet. I worried about how I could do more and do it better.

One day, on the healing couch in my apartment, Boz-enka didn't want to wake up and had this dream. She said, "I was in a strange unknown place. Miles and miles of land was covered with bricks. There were huge rocks and rusty nails, rotting timber and fallen trees. I knew there was beautiful fertile land under that terrible mess and I knew I must make a garden of it. The urge was very strong and overwhelming, but it was a hard and almost impossible job for one person. Then people I had known and loved appeared suddenly. My dear mother was among them. We worked endlessly, the blisters on our hands were full of blood. We pulled, we carried, we cried. It was madness. One by one the people walked away, my mother was the last one to leave. Tears ran down my face and I felt as if I was alone in the universe. Suddenly I felt the presence of my grandfather. "Nobody can clear the land," he said. "You only have to plant a seed."

"I looked down and there was one tiny seed of a sweet pea in my left hand. Grandfather had gone. It was hours before I was able to clear the rubbish and get down to the soil. There was just enough for one small seed. Immediately a tiny plant started to grow. It had one leaf, then two, then three, then incredibly, one hundred. It was growing over rocks and bricks and blanketing the rotting timber. I saw the power of the seed as it grew more and more. An ocean of sweet peas covered the land and blossomed in white, purple, red and pink. The power of the seed and the power of beginning—there are no words to describe it."

Boz-enka's dream encouraged me to plant the seed by writing down all the information that may be of value to anyone working with people who are suffering.

That was a message to me. As I worked seven days a week, trying to help people that doctors had given up on it seemed that those efforts were not enough. Why not plant a seed I thought, and let people know that love, kindness and prayer can do what seems impossible. The power of seed, the power of beginning, let us experience it together.

While writing this story I have had a telephone call from Annette. She has been totally blind for a number of months and was told that nothing could be done for her. She came for three treatments and has had absentee healings a few times. Her sight is gradually improving. She can now see well enough to read a newspaper.

The North Island of New Zealand

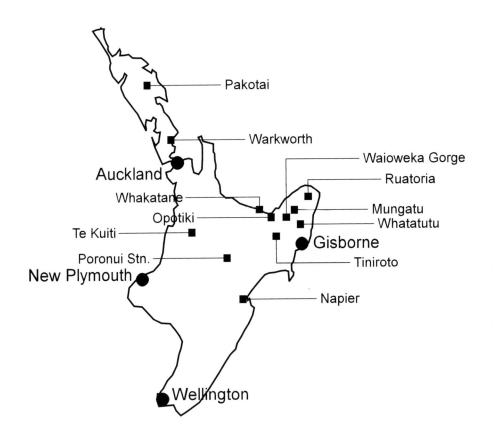

Locations of the stories in Part 1

PART 1—Memories of an old horseman

These stories are included because people in other countries wanted to know where the healing had been learnt. Had I spent all my life in a monastery or had I travelled the world learning from healers? What education did I have for this work? I have learned from other people, animals and my own experience. In this section I talk about out some of the things I learnt and some of the people I admired as I grew up.

Examples of the People I Have Known

Bill O'Mera

(Whatatutu, New Zealand)

When I was born at Whatatutu, New Zealand, in 1914, Bill O'Mera lived just across some paddocks from my home. He was an old man then and I thought he had lived forever.

He was a man of few words and his word was his bond. He was greatly respected by everyone, especially the children of the district, and was willing to give advice or listen to problems of all children learning to ride and work with their animals.

He had great love and respect for all living things and I am sure his influence helped to shape my outlook on life.

He owned about twenty acres of land where the Mangatu Pa stands today and ran a boarding house (Pa designates a Maori village). On his land he grew all his own fruit and vegetables, milked cows, raised hens and kept bees. As school children we found out all about the bees he used to keep in his orchard—we walked past it twice a day to and from school.

Bees teaching a lesson and protecting fruit

There was little money there in those days, but thousands of sheep and cattle were being driven to market past Bill's place every year. All drovers, swaggers and people travelling by buggy used to stay the night with Bill O'Mera. (Swaggers were people who walked from place to place with everything they owned on their back.) The ones with no money often used to do small jobs around the farm.

There used to be a big shed on Mr. O'Mera's farm. It was big enough to drive a buggy and team of horses into. There were stalls there to shelter the horses and other animals at night. It had a big loft above and separate chutes to slide the food down to the feed boxes below.

His animals and poultry were always in the best of condition and he was always willing to share his knowledge with anyone who was looking for information about rearing healthy stock or plants.

Bill O'Mera was a well known horseman and a good judge of horses and people. He used to ride up until a few years before he died. He bred some good horses and used to have my brother Ken, and other horsemen, ride them in the horse sports for him.

I will say once again he had the greatest respect for all living things and I can honestly say that every animal he owned was always well fed and in the best of condition. Even today when I see good stock I find myself comparing them with Bill O'Mera's animals.

Bill O'Mera was a bachelor all the time I knew him. I believe he went to a Catholic hospital before he died and have since heard that he left everything he owned to the Catholic Church. While I was in the Mater Hospital in Auckland being looked after so wonderfully by the Catholic nuns, I could understand how he could leave everything to these people, who were so kind and caring. It is nice to think that before he died he would have received some of the same kindness and caring which he had given so freely, to every one of God's creatures that he came in contact with.

No man ever had more kindness and concern for any of God's creatures than Bill O'Mera. I now realise that it was my admiration for him and his influence on me that guided me to put my own experiences in writing to let people know the value of love and respect for all living things.

Tommy Hopper

Tommy Hopper was another man that I learnt a lot from. As a boy he came out from England to a strange country where he knew no one. He was determined to get work and be successful and—some day—bring his mother and brother out to New Zealand to live. He was a thin small boy and went to the toughest area in the back blocks to try to find work. He arrived at Whatatutu where all the roads were river beds.

He was walking up a river bed carrying a small suitcase containing all the belongings he had in the world, when two big burly men pulled up in a wagon and offered him a ride. When asked where he was going, he said he had heard of a Harry Campbell who was always wanting workers. They thought this was a great joke and told him there was a steady stream of men going up for work one week, then coming back down again the next. They said, "You might get work there, but you won't last one day."

They didn't deter him. He went all the way up and arrived at the station where there were many big powerful men waiting for the wagon to get their mail. They all had a great laugh when they heard this boy was going to ask for work. When he finally got into the boss's office, the boss looked at him and said, "Well what can I do for you?" When Tommy said, "I am looking for work," the boss replied, "Will you just tell me how much you know about running half wild cattle and sheep in this sort of country?" Tommy said, "I don't know anything, but am willing to learn."

Camp oven

The boss replied, "You are just the man I've been looking for. See all those men out there? They all think they know everything already, so they will never learn. You can start now and I will give you an old horse and an old dog. If you watch them carefully they will teach you more than you can ever get out of a book. Always trust your horse. If you get caught in a flooded river your horse will take you to where you can get into a bend in the river. Just go with the current instead of going against it and your horse will carry you safely out on the other side. Watch your dog at all times when driving or shifting stock. The dog will know what you want to do so watch him so you can work together."

The other men never knew what Tommy had done to be able to get that job and keep it for many years. He finished up managing some of those big stations, then owned land of his own. He finally brought his mother and brother out to live with him.

Tommy was a very practical man and used to stay with me at Poronui Station. He suffered a lot from effects of war wounds. To see him moving around the kitchen you would think he would hardly be able to go outside and back.

Sometimes you would meet him in the hills five miles from the homestead carrying a rifle; or find a message on a gate written in deer's blood using a bullet as a pen, to say there was some fresh meat under a tree up the hill for us to collect.

He often cooked the meals for 3 or more men. One night we came home and there was one pot on the stove and 3 plates, knives and forks and mugs on the table. He asked would we like some soup and dished this up from the pot. Then we had meat, vegetables and doughboys from the same pot. Then dessert with doughboys and golden syrup from the same pot on the same plate. He said if a woman cooked a 3 course meal like this she would use many pots, pans and basins, all of which would have to be washed up afterwards.

It was a very satisfying and welcome meal and there were no complaints of only one plate each to wash plus one pot.

The men picked for the top jobs managing or owning those big hill country stations were not chosen for their academic qualities. They were chosen because they were able to work with nature and had respect for their animals and the men working under them. The main thing seemed to be being able to work with nature and get the urgent jobs done while the weather was right, even if it meant working long hours, then doing maintenance work in the other times.

What Tommy was learning there from his old horse and dog, about working with nature and not against it, was the same lesson as I had been learning from the time we learnt to walk and ride at the same time.

Jack Casey

I was privileged to have lived next door to Jack Casey who was recognised as the best horseman in the area. There seemed to be hundreds of horses ridden or driven past our house every day, but nobody took any notice. But when Jack Casey went past, everyone in the family went to watch. He was always riding a young horse that he was educating. The horse always moved so freely and moved with its head high, and horse and rider moved as one, in perfect harmony together. There were also big mobs of sheep and cattle driven past the house. Sometimes the drovers moving the stock would be having trouble with half wild cattle just brought out of the bush.

One day there was a wild cow that had broken away from a mob when Jack Casey was coming up the road. He and his horse stopped the cow in the middle of the road and turned it back. It jumped down a bank into a stream, but horse and rider were there to block it at every move. Then the cow rushed across the road and jumped over a high seven-wire fence. The horse and rider were there with it, turning the cow in a circle and at a full gallop cow, horse and rider all came back over the fence together. Then with a few extra bites from the horse, the cow went down the road back to the mob and horse and rider moved on down the road as if nothing had happened.

Jack was riding in a light English saddle and never gave any indication that he was in control of the horse—they just moved as one in perfect harmony. I was privileged to see him do this sort of thing many times. He had broken in many hundreds of horses in that area and each one was a gentle and perfectly mannered hack for the rest of its life.

I was nine years old when Jack died in 1923, but he left an impression on my mind that will be there always. Without words he showed me by his example the importance of love, kindness and respect for all living things.

Knowing him meant more to me than I can ever explain.

Tommy Edwards

Another rider worth mentioning was Tommy Edwards, a Maori boy from Whatatutu. He would take out almost any horse even if it had only been ridden two or three times and had never seen a jump before. He would go to a hunt and jump full seven-wire fences all day and never put a foot wrong. For a start he would hold back a bit until others had jumped the fence and were galloping away on the other side. All young horses want to follow when other horses are galloping. Then he would let his horse go and clear the fence with feet to spare. Tommy never kept any horses of his own; he just loved starting off a young horse.

Like many good horsemen Tommy was never in the limelight and was never interested in riding made horses in competitions year after year ("Made horses" means educated and trained by someone else). He and I worked together often breaking in big mobs of twenty to thirty in one place. He couldn't hide his love for young horses and they responded by learning very quickly. Many of the best horses in the country owe their success to people like Tommy who gave them so much kindness and consideration in their early stages of education.

Tommy Edwards on Whisky at Puha

Ken and Ann Brown

Ken Brown and his wife Ann are (in my opinion) the most capable horse people in New Zealand. They break in and train all their horses themselves. Ken rides racehorses and steeplechasers in competitions. They both come from long lines of very capable and respected horse people. Ken has probably bred, trained, ridden and won on more horses than anyone else in New Zealand.

Their horses are not kept in yards, but are run out in the paddocks and trained over the hills. They both know how much that freedom means to a horse. Before they were married, Ann (nee Frazer) had an outstanding horse called Trooper. In most show rings in New Zealand they won champion hack (similar to dressage), champion hunter and many other jumping events—on the same day! When Mark Todd won his first world championship event he said he had learnt more from Ann and Ken Brown than from anyone else. They have both inherited so much knowledge and love and respect and feeling for their animals that it is no wonder they are so successful.

Now that so many people spend all their time in cars or offices or with some kind of mechanical machine and live in cities with very little contact with nature, it is no wonder that when they do get on a horse they treat it like a mechanical toy and not like a friend to share their life with. We were really sharing our lives with these animals and relied on them completely for our everyday survival. We knew they would risk their lives for us if we were in real danger. This gave us great respect for our horses and our dogs and we were well rewarded when we treated them with kindness and respect.

Dinie the champion camp draughter

The old way of learning to ride

(Whatatutu, New Zealand)

We learned to ride on quiet horses that had been ridden all day, every day, for many years. Some had spent almost all their lives in harness or packing big loads over the hills. Some were as quiet and gentle as it was possible to be—totally different from horses that were only ridden for a few hours a week.

The situation was much different than it is today. As babies we were often carried on the front or back of someone on a horse. That is why I say we learnt to ride and walk almost at the same time.

Many children just loved their horses and could find all sorts of ways to get on a horse's back when there was nobody there to lift them on. The method used most often was to get the horse near a fence or gate then climb on from the gate. But many horses would let you spend hours climbing up onto a gate then move away just enough so you couldn't get on their back.

Getting into position

When there were two children, it was much easier. You could get the horse behind the gate and open it wide and have the horse between the gate and the fence. That way, he couldn't move sideways until you were on his back.

Leading by the leg

Where there is a will, there is a way—and children always found some way of catching their horse to be ridden. One child I knew used to take the bridle out into the paddock and spread it out in front of the horse where it was eating grass. Then he would just wait until the horse moved forwards and put its foot into the bridle. He would then gather up the bridle over his shoulder and lead the horse, by its front leg, home to his mother. She would then put the bridle on and lift him onto the horse's back. He would stay there for many hours just being with the horse while it fed its way around the paddock.

Some other children used to take a few pieces of carrots down to where the horse was feeding and put them down in front of the horse. While he had his head down, one child would climb onto his neck. Then, when he lifted his head, they would crawl along his neck onto his back. Then they would put down more pieces of carrot and the next boy would get onto the horse's neck, crawling onto its back in the same way. Many times they would slip off again while trying to turn around on his back to face the right way!

Mounting by the neck

Sometimes they would put a bridle on while his head was down so they could try to steer him the way they wanted to go. Other times they were content to just sit on his back while the horse fed around the paddock.

There was one thing we learnt—it was a long way down to the ground from some of those big horses! Especially if they walked too fast downhill and you slipped off and landed with another child or two on top of you!

Most of these were old horses, almost retired from hard work, but they seemed to get as much pleasure out of the love and close contact with the children as the children got from them. They really had learnt love and respect for each other.

After riding bareback for many years—wherever they wanted to go—by the time these children grew up they had learnt perfect balance. Horse and rider would move as one.

The children who learnt to ride in this way would now be the parents or grandparents of the top New Zealand horsemen of today.

My schooling

(Whatatutu, New Zealand)

Friends for life

The school I attended was in Whatatutu at the foothills of Raukumara ranges. On the way to school we could see Mt Mangahamia, Mt Arowhana and Mt Hikurangi. Mt Hikurangi is the first place in this world for the sun to rise on every day of the year. It is in the back blocks of the East Cape of New Zealand about 30 miles from Gisborne. It seemed to be in the back blocks in those days (around 1918) because the only access to Gisborne from Whatatutu was by horse and coach to the nearest train at Puha. Then it took what seemed like ages to go on to Gisborne and back, with the train stopping at every little siding along the way. These stations were Te Karaka, Kaiteratahi, Ormond, Waerenga-a-hika and Makaraka. It was a whole day's outing just to make a round trip.

There were very few cars in New Zealand when I was first at school. Most kids walked or rode to school bareback and there is no better way to learn balance than years of bareback riding in rough country. Until I was twelve years old all of my riding was done bareback.

Learning from nature

Learning from the Maoris

(Whatatutu, New Zealand)

Fifty percent of the students at Whatatutu School were Maori, but they were never allowed to speak Maori in school. There was never a chance to learn their language, or anything about their culture. They just kept all that to themselves.

Many of the old Maoris had never been to school, but we learnt a lot by the example they set. Their word was their bond. They were honest people and had respect for each other and all living things. All the younger people had the greatest respect for the old Maoris. They earned that respect by being what they were, with their word as their bond that would never be broken; and for their kindness towards anyone or any sick animal that needed help.

My parents used to say that if you did a good turn towards a Maori you had a friend for life. One story I remember was when my mother was alone in the house when some Maoris were singing Christmas carols around the district. They didn't come right to the house because a baby was crying inside. The only way my mother knew they were there was because they had a violin played by Bill Kapeta and were playing and singing lullabies outside until the baby went to sleep. "Go to sleep my baby, close your pretty eyes. The angels are up above you...."

Bringing home the bacon at Te Hoi

Learning from animals and nature

(North Island, New Zealand)

After school I used to work with Ken Garmnsway who used to break in horses all around the area. He would ride them once or twice then let me ride them to give them experience at cantering in a figure eight and to get them used to being ridden.

The worst part of the job was when they were ready to be shod. It would be my job to take them to the blacksmith Dan Anderson for their first set of shoes. I would have to stand there and hold them. Sometimes I would need to hold horses all day when there were a lot to be done. The experience taught me at an early age the value of getting a horse to respond to a gentle touch.

Every weekend was spent on horseback up and down the riverbeds, always shifting some kind of stock from one place to another. So at the weekends we were learning a lot about living with nature and learning from the animals we were in contact with.

We were always taught to trust our horse's judgment if we were in a flooded river or trying to find our way home on a dark night. We were also taught never to waste anything because even a crumb of bread was a nice meal to a cold hungry little bird. We learnt that if you were kind to an animal they would never forget and the same if you were cruel to them.

Because I wanted to be with nature and with the people who worked close to nature, I left school at the age of 14 and went away on a cattle drive. The drive went through the Waioeka Gorge from Gisborne to Opotiki and Whakatane before that area was open to traffic. I never went back to school.

Wild horses caught the previous day at Rangitaiki

From then on all of my time was spent on big back-country farms in many parts of New Zealand. That was where I got my real education—the knowledge gained from living with respect for nature and all living things; or should I say working with nature and all living things and not working against them.

Marie Howard on Paint at Rangitaiki

This knowledge was a great help later in life in managing big areas of land being developed into farmland, handling a big staff, handling thousands of sheep and cattle, and in keeping a team of approximately five dogs for working stock.

Pride comes before a fall

(Whatatutu, New Zealand)

At the age of thirteen, with other older boys including Frank and Charlie Gaukroger, we found out we could jump seven-wire fences. These were strained very tight and had many battens or droppers between each post. On the way home from school, instead of walking on the road, we would go through the paddocks and jump every fence on the way.

One day when getting near home there was a brand new fence that had been built over the week end. My brother Ken was walking up the road so I called him over to watch me jump this fence which was much higher than the rest. He tried to tell me this one was too high, but I said, "No, you watch, I can jump it." The ground was much lower on one side and when I did jump my foot just touched the top wire and I landed very heavily on my side and both knees banged together. This was very painful and I was feeling very sorry for myself. Then Ken said, "Pride always comes before a fall."

This didn't make me feel one bit better but it was a lesson I never forgot. Never again did I ever talk about what I was going to do. I would just quietly try to do what I wanted to do, then if I was unsuccessful it didn't matter, but if I was successful, I didn't need to say one word as others would say all that was necessary.

In this area there were hundreds of horses and there would occasionally be a horse that some people said could not be ridden. Often people with great reputations would come for miles and were willing to bet they could ride any horse. A lot of people would gather to see how they would succeed or to put money on the horse or the rider.

More often than not they would be unsuccessful. I found that by not saying a word and going there quietly and at least having a try, then giving it everything I had, it wouldn't matter if I didn't succeed. Then if they wanted to, other people could talk later and I didn't need to say a word.

Many of these horses just behaved like ladies' hacks and wanted to follow me everywhere afterwards.

As I have often told people, if you want to help someone, at least try. When you do try things that may seem impossible, you will often be amazed at the results, even when there doesn't seem to be any chance of success. Especially when you are trying to help some other living thing there seems to be a guiding angel there to help you.

Breaking in or educating horses

(North Island, New Zealand)

For six years after leaving school I did droving (herding) and mustering (rounding up) always riding young horses, mostly to quieten them down for other people. Then for 13 years I worked full-time breaking in horses and used to do over 200 each year.

The majority of the horses were three years old or more and had never been touched or had a rope on them. In each mob (herd) there would be one or two horses that people had tried to break in and failed. However, I found that with the right treatment they all responded and became quiet.

All the farmers in the area bred their own horses. These horses were castrated at one year then left together on the highest roughest hills on the farm to make them sure footed under rough conditions. When they were yarded (corralled) at three years old, they were just like wild horses that had never been in a yard or near a man in their lives. Most mobs were five to twenty on each farm. My job was to break them in or educate them, so they would be quiet enough for anyone to ride.

This work paid just a bit better than normal stockmen's wages. People used to pay two pounds each for breaking in a horse and ten shillings to shoe them.

Drawing of a wild stallion at Rangitaiki

Breaking in approximately 200 horses every year for 13 years, including all the ones other people had tried to break in and failed, I learnt a lot about how a wild animal would respond to kindness and respect and how they remembered that kindness. Many times I was given a horse that others had been unable to break. I would only have to ride it once or twice and it would be quiet for anyone to ride for the rest of its life.

By the time I was eighteen I had learnt that any bucking horse could be ridden much more easily by balance alone, sitting completely relaxed and loose in the saddle, where there was room for movement between the rider and the saddle and the horse. Just a gentle touch on the reins was enough to help you keep your balance, but not enough for the horse to be able to pull you off balance.

During this time I had many falls from horses. They sometimes went crazy at first and fell over banks or over backwards. Sometimes gear would break. One horse broke the crupper and pulled the saddle over its head even though there was a new surcingle (cinch) and as the saddle came over its head with the surcingle still intact it also took the bridle off so I was sitting on a rocky river bed on the saddle and the horse had gone free with nothing on.

By the time I was twenty-three I had won first prize in the New Zealand Rodeo Riding Championship twice and received eight pounds prize money each time. There wasn't the big money there is today for this type of work.

I always had more than I could do breaking in other peoples horses, and then went on to manage big blocks of land until I got some land of my own.

A "Major" lesson

(Tiniroto, New Zealand)

While doing this work only one horse ever bucked me off or threw me right out of the saddle when I was doing my best to stay there. He was a big strong horse with a very quiet nature, but very lazy. Later he was named Major and was owned by Toby Richardson of Tiniroto.

The first time I rode Major I just couldn't get him to go out of a slow walk. So next time I decided to use a stick to move him along a bit faster and show him who was boss. I soon found out who was boss. He exploded in mid-air and swapped ends the first two bucks and did a lot of jerking on the way up on the third one. I am not sure what he did on the way down because he had decided to land somewhere else when we got back to earth.

He stood very quietly while I got on again and told him in no uncertain terms that was just a fluke and that he would soon find out that no horse could do that to me. In four seconds he had done it again! I realised that I wasn't as good a rider as I thought I was, or he was a better bucker than I was a rider, but there was no way I was going to let him know that. So I took him into a small muddy yard that was very slippery and let him go around at his own pace until he found out how slippery it was. Then I used a soft poplar stick to hurry him along. The stick had plenty of leaves and twigs so that it would make a lot of noise and wouldn't hurt much.

Mangapoiki Station

The slippery ground took a lot of the sting out of his bucking, but he was still pretty rough. We managed to stay together so I then took him into a bigger slippery yard and gave him a good work out. In an hour or so I could get him cantering in a figure eight.

He turned out to be a nice quiet horse and even before he had been ridden with a saddle, he would stand while you jumped on his back and you could slide off his tail without fear of being kicked. He really was a good horse and never ever bucked again. He also turned out to be a good jumper.

Many years later I heard that Major wasn't ridden for two years after he was broken in. Then someone—who didn't know his reputation as a bucker—rode him for a year, but when he heard how Major had been able to buck, never rode him again. The next man who got him rode him to the hunts for many weeks before someone told him what a good bucker he had been—so he never rode him again either, but sold him to someone else.

I had been so annoyed about being bucked off twice by one horse that I hadn't thought of keeping Major for a top rodeo horse. But Major never did buck again and I am sure he only did it this once to teach me a lesson. A horse *could* buck me off!

One thing I learnt was that the horses that had never been touched by anyone else were much easier to educate because they had never learnt any bad habits and were more willing to respond to a gentle touch and kindness. Another very important thing was to always reward them with a pat or a stroke when they did something right. Horses learn much quicker with kindness and respect than by being punished when they do something wrong.

The sparrow hawk

(Whatatutu, New Zealand)

While working in cattle yards on the side of a big hill where there was a cliff below us, and high bush covered hills reaching to the clouds above, a sparrow

Te Rata Station at Whatatutu

hawk appeared in the sky and started making a terrific noise. It was flying around in circles just below the clouds and continued to screech out for some time. Then another bird came from the cliffs below us and started flying around in circles just level to where we were working. Every time the one in the clouds would screech out, the one level with us would answer.

Then the one in the clouds dropped something which came down close to where we were. As it got close, the bird from below came over to catch it and we could see that it was a dead rat. The second bird took it back to its nest somewhere below us at the base of the cliff.

The bird in the clouds flew back into the bush to carry on hunting. Later on when he had caught something else high up in the mountains and bush, he would just fly out on a level flight and allow gravity to take the meal down to his mate, who could then take it to the sheltered nest down below.

They were getting the maximum amount of help from nature using gravity to the best advantage to get food home with the least amount of effort. The bird doing the hunting just had short level flights to get food from the bush to its nest thousands of feet below and return to the job of hunting.

Birds and animals of every description don't only work with nature, but use it to their best advantage in every way possible. God and nature will help us and guide us if we are willing to listen and learn.

Gaining from a dog's instincts

(North Island, New Zealand)

I never bought a dog, but would take dogs that other people said were no good—every one started to work for me straight-away without hesitation, some within five minutes while the previous owner was still there. By finding out what each dog wanted to do by instinct, I let him specialise

Happy people have happy dogs

in doing that job. This way they were just developing the way they wanted to and it was so easy for me and for them.

All my dogs turned out to be top performers. While other people had tried to make these dogs do what wasn't in their instinct to do, I was just working with the animals and not against them.

The little dog

(Rangitikei, New Zealand)

Where I lived, a quick solution to a problem often meant the difference between life and death. This day it was my life on the line and a quick definite decision had to be made.

My dogs and I were out in the open country miles from anywhere when the dogs bailed up a huge wild pig. The pig was the size of a lion and had been doing a lot of damage to newborn animals for a long period and had always managed to keep out of sight. He had long razor sharp tusks and the dogs were keeping just out of reach.

There was only one bullet in my light .22 rifle and the pig's skull was so tough that the bullet just flattened out on the outside of his forehead. There and then he decided I was the cause of his trouble and he was going to get me.

My older dogs were trained to handle the pig if it galloped towards me. They would get in close alongside the pig and both grab an ear at the same time. As long as they could both hang on, he couldn't hurt either one. But he only came at a trot and could swing either way very quickly so they couldn't grab him.

There were no trees around large enough to climb, only a lot of small saplings. So my best hope was to hold on to a tree and keep in an upright position and hope to be able to kick him on the nose or get my foot in his mouth to give the dogs a chance to grab him. Even if this did work, I couldn't help thinking there would be a lot of blood lost and wondered how I would get back to where my horse was.

There were two big dogs with me and a little female fox terrier who had gone over the hill following another pig. After calling her back to help, she came galloping down the hill, summed up the position and made a split second decision and without slacking her pace, took a flying leap in behind the big pig and fastened her sharp teeth into his testicles. The pain and shock made the pig sit down and this is all that was needed to allow the other dogs to get a good hold, one behind each ear.

This allowed me to get hold of his tail and get my belt around his hind leg so that if he did get away from the dogs, he wouldn't be able to turn to face me to attack. Then it was possible to get him on his back and finish him off with a knife.

Quick decision that saved a life

As it happened, the pig was the only one who lost any blood. But if that little dog hadn't made a quick decision and got right to the point, it may have been a different story or no story at all.

The old dog

(Warkworth, New Zealand)

At one time we were in the process of shifting (moving) from one farm to another to get nearer to the city, beaches and the school. With a slow old truck I was shifting one load of cattle every night to avoid most of the traffic. It was necessary to leave in the evening and arrive at the other farm about midnight.

As my dog had been hurt while working cattle, I was unable to take him with me. I wanted to shift the cattle into the back paddock because we weren't sure how secure the gates were in the front area. Also, some gates had been left open by people walking through. I didn't know how it would be possible to shift them over two small bridges to the back paddock in the dark, but thought there would be some way even if it did take a long time. It was a wet, misty night and I didn't arrive there until 1:30 in the morning.

When the truck was backed into the yard to unload the cattle, there was an old dog standing in the headlights. I went and patted him and said, "I know what you are here for." He seemed just as pleased to see me as I was to see him. After we had unloaded the cattle it was pitch dark and I couldn't see a thing. So I followed the fence around to open the gate and the dog followed the cattle. Every time I wanted to let him know where I was, I would give a whistle. Then he would bark to let me know where he and the cattle were, then bring them towards me. Using this method we managed to shift the cattle through three paddocks and over two bridges in complete darkness.

When we got back to the truck I thanked him and shared a piece of bread with him. Like most dogs, he wanted to come home with me, but as I thought he belonged to some local farmer, I had to tell him to stay behind. We worked so well together, just as if we had been working together all our lives so I felt very sad to go away and leave him. I have thought many times since that it was no coincidence that he happened to be there on that cold wet night—just at the moment he was needed—when he should have been cuddled down in a nice warm sheltered spot somewhere.

When we finally shifted down there to live, I inquired all around the district, but nobody knew of a dog like the one I described. I had never seen him before that day, and have never seen him since, but at that time there was a very strong bond between us. This dog was using all the

Can't I come with you?

powers I didn't have just to help me. He had the ability to see much better in the dark, his sense of smell told him if any cattle had stopped behind, and he was able to hear when any cattle were going the wrong way and would be there to stop them.

Animals have so much more ability in so many ways that it is a pity that more of us are not willing to learn from them. If I had been shifting stock out of a flooded river or away from a bush fire, that dog would have worked until he dropped or even risked his life just because I had shown him a bit of respect. If we all showed more respect for each other, what a different world it would be!

Writing in peace with nature

PART 2—Respect for all living things

Birds' messages

(Pakotai, New Zealand)

There have been hundreds of copies requested and distributed of the story of the first little bird we healed and the story has been read out in churches in Canada and in the U.S.A.

Since then people from almost every nationality have told me stories of how a bird brought them nearer to God and to nature. One was an Indian man in Canada who was driving home one night on a narrow rough road when a cat chased a Blue Jay in front of his car. He jammed on the brakes but the bird seemed to have been hit and just stood on the road.

After picking it up and leaving it on a post, he was having trouble opening the door of his car. The bird flew after him and landed on his arm and wouldn't go away. The bird was quite capable of flying but just wouldn't leave. Every time he put it on the post and went to leave it, it would fly back and get into the car. Finally they had to take it home and it has lived with them ever since. They felt that God had sent them that bird for a reason, probably for protection. It may even have protected them from an accident further along the road.

Another story is from a lady living in a high building in New York. Her husband was undergoing an operation for cancer and the doctors didn't think there was much chance of him surviving the operation.

She was alone in the room 10 stories up praying all the time and suddenly there was a great peace and a little bird landed on her window and was looking right at her and singing. She said she knew then without any doubt that her husband was going to recover and in fact he did recover after the operation.

Messages coming without words

Another lady in Canada was on her way into town when she stopped where a bird was run over on the road and shifted it to the side of the road. When she was driving home again she thought it wasn't far enough off the road so she stopped again and shifted it right back under some bushes. When she got into the car to drive away there were birds singing to her and saying thanks. Their thanks to God for a little bit of kindness couldn't have been said more plainly.

A lady in New Zealand who had just returned home from an operation, was home alone and praying to God for a complete recovery when a little Fantail came and sat on her window sill. It used to come every day and when it's baby was able to fly enough it used to bring her baby to give this lady support and comfort.

As long as she remembers the visit by this bird and her baby she will always be close to God and nature and be in the right frame of mind to overcome anything.

Fantail.
Can you share Nature with me?

A person from Chicago had heard the story about the little bird we had healed and he asked me to go over there to do some healing, because he thought a person who would take some time to work on a little bird must have some kindness in him. He was from the Johnny Coleman's church where three thousand people attend every Sunday. At the invitation of the elder who had heard about the little bird story I flew to Chicago and stayed at a Holiday Inn. Johnny and some of the elders from the church came to the Holiday Inn the next day for healing. The man who asked us to come was looking out the window while healing was in progress and birds came from every direction until there were estimated to be 400 there and they all sat in two trees just outside the window. A story from him about what he had seen is included later in this book.

Living at ground level

(Calgary, Alberta)

While in Canada there was a phone call on December 17, 1991 from New Zealand asking if I would give help with healing prayers for Marie who was in hospital in a coma dying of two brain tumours. She was expected to die before Christmas.

This phone call was 2.30 AM so I sent healing to Marie straight away and could feel the two tumours and removed them from her spiritual body. Two days later Peter rang back to say Marie's pain had all gone and she was sitting up in bed having a meal and was going home for Christmas. Marie has had two children since and is still free of the tumours.

When Peter called again later he mentioned during the conversation that many psychic people were expecting big spiritual changes in the Southern Hemisphere on the 21st of June of 1992 and they were going to sit on the hills all night waiting for the changes. He also asked if I would see if there were any changes in the North. Later I learnt that on June 21st people had sat up on the hills in New Zealand looking towards the sky waiting for spiritual changes but had not felt or seen anything. The only thing that had been recorded was that many people had seen birds of every type coming together in mobs and forming big circles and singing to each other. Nobody had thought to make a video of them which was a pity, because Indians and people who have lived with nature all their lives, would have known what the message was that they were trying to give us.

Smells like the man who helped me once

One Maori prophet said the people were all looking in the wrong place for the changes. They were coming from the earth and working up through everything.

I told this story to some ministers of the church in Missouri because they had been saying every week that everyone should go to church every Sunday and all pray together and ask to be part of God and that then, all people could become like God, and all human beings would be one big family.

After telling them this bird story I said, "You think if you all pray in church God will come down to meet you half way and all human beings will become one big happy family. It's not like that, because when you just focus on human beings you are considering only a small part of the whole." Human beings wouldn't be anything without the rest of the living things. All people should realise every living thing is part of God's family, and have love and respect for every other part and each other.

Then I was guided to say, "If we all lived at ground level with love and respect for each other, and all living things, we wouldn't have to pray and ask God for anything because he would be there with us." Don't pray and tell God what you want him to do for you, ask him what you can do for him, what you can do to help all living things and all he created.

One minister thanked me for what I had said and never mentioned "all human beings" again but said "all living things."

When a little seed wants to be a big fruit tree it doesn't say God please make me into a big fruit tree and become one. First it has to get to earth to the soil that has been worked on by worms and all sorts of other insects. Then it has to have the sun and rain. Next when it starts to grow there are bugs and insects that will try to destroy it.

Birds will help it by keeping the bugs away. Then as it grows larger, small animals will feed on its young shoots so it will have to produce more than it needs to be able to survive. As time goes on flowers will appear, but they are no use unless the bees and other insects come to help. By this time larger animals are feeding off the lower branches and those animals leave manure which give it more strength to survive.

Finally it is producing fruit which becomes food, and leaves which provide shelter and protection for many sorts of animals, insects and birds.

Each one of these things was created by God for a purpose and was guided by God while it was doing its job. Humans have to also learn to be part of God's family and not think they are superior and can do without everything else and survive on their own.

Spruce Meadows

(Calgary, Alberta)

Spruce Meadows is a horse competition held annually just outside Calgary, Alberta, Canada. This letter relates the experience of being a visitor at this competition.

To The Southern Family and Staff

Dear Nancy

I was at Spruce Meadows the other day when you were having jumping competitions for horses and riders from all over the world, but you were all so busy with organising and the competitions that there was not time to talk to you.

It was a wonderful day out there and everyone seemed to be enjoying themselves so much. What impressed me most was the love, kindness and respect everywhere, among the pensioners and handicapped on the free bus, the people in wheelchairs on the ground and the blind man I was talking to. They were all having a wonderful day. The fact that they were all able to be right there in those beautiful surroundings, and to be able to see and hear all that was going on and see and meet all those horses and riders from other countries competing at world class level, meant more than you can possibly imagine to those old disabled people.

Animal lovers were drawn to Spruce Meadows, and they all live close to God whether they know it or not. So there was a feeling there of belonging to something wonderful.

Jesus himself was born in a stable among the animals so what better place could you get for those disabled people to feel close to Jesus and nature than in your stables where they see all those beautiful horses that have had so much love and kindness given to them and a person can't go near them without feeling some of that love and respect that has been given to them so freely.

The first day I met you, your son Karl and your Grandfather, I knew that the whole organisation had been built up on hard work, honesty, and respect for others and all living things. It is wonderful to see that so many people are receiving more pleasure than you could possibly imagine just from the privilege of being out there for a day.

For you people who are working out there all the time it may not seem like much, but for someone who has been sitting in a wheelchair all winter, not knowing if they would ever be out in the fresh air again, being at Spruce Meadows must have felt like being in heaven for a few hours. After those top horses and horsemen are brought together from all over the world to compete they cannot go back to their own countries without taking some of the love, kindness and respect that they have experienced while they have been here with them.

We should be grateful to God for all we have, and it is up to each one of us to do all we can to bring honesty and respect back into the community. Just by doing what you are, you are all doing more than your share, and we know how much hard work and time it takes to run such a big organisation

Someone wrote in an old Rodeo Cowboy's bible that had been given to me, "What you are is god's gift to you, what you make of yourself is your gift to god."

The differences between Spruce Meadows and most of the big churches is that no matter how poor you are or how sick, or how much you need help, or how disabled, or what losses you have had in the family, Spruce Meadows does not judge, nor do they expect monetary return. The other churches spend so much time asking for money for one thing or another and saying the more you give the more you will receive, this embarrasses the people who haven't anything to give, especially when they went there hoping to get some help. When they say give, they don't say give to the sick and poor or people who haven't any, they expect you to give only to them.

At Spruce Meadows you didn't ask for anything. I am sure many of those old disabled people and everyone else who had rides on the free buses running from Calgary to Spruce Meadows every hour all day, went home from there feeling closer to God and nature than they have after leaving some of the churches.

ON BEHALF OF ALL THOSE DISABLED PEOPLE WE GIVE OUR LOVE AND RESPECT AND SAY MAY GOD BLESS YOU ALL

Rod Campbell

Feeling part of nature

This feeling comes more easily when you are the only person within many miles and you are out in the bush or mountains, where there is no sign of anything made by man; where there are only wild animals, birds and insects and trees, shrubs, grass and flowers and new buds and leaves on the trees and birds busy looking for a place to start building their nests. Occasionally there will be a shower of rain and some wind. This is all part of God's pattern so we can all survive and live in harmony together. Then you can feel a great love and respect for all those living things that is overwhelming, and is so strong and powerful that it cannot be described. That is when you feel so small and unimportant, no more important than the smallest seed or the smallest insect. All wild animals and people who have lived close to nature can feel the power of the love and respect that there is between all living things and know that it is something so powerful that we just don't know what it is.

The amount of healing that goes on out there among all living things is unbelievable; animals and birds that have had accidents, then recovered; and trees that have been damaged by flood, storm or fire, then started to grow again. Often you see a whole hillside of bush that has slipped away, but after a few years, new forests have grown and left trees, shrubs and flowers just as beautiful as before.

It is the love and healing power that brings all living things together each year in order that their sperm or seeds can reproduce another crop of living things into the world, so we can all go on living in harmony with love and respect for each other. This love and healing power can be passed on to help each other and all living things provided it is given unconditionally for no recognition or reward.

Sign from Nature

It has been proven and recorded hundreds of times, that this power can be passed on to heal all kinds of diseases and ailments in people, after the doctors have told them they only have a week or so to live and there is nothing medical science can do for them. There are many children, nurses and social workers who have this gift in various stages and could develop it if they had any encouragement, but they do not get any, because it is not written in books or taught in schools or medical teaching.

Many medical doctors have used this healing energy in one way or another to help people. In the USA many medical doctors have lost their licences to practice by being involved with this healing energy. The reason for this is that the medical association in the USA is only interested in the methods of treatment of the association and does not wish to recognise the saving of lives by other treatment practices. It has been shown many thousands of times that people beyond the help of standard medical procedures have been helped by healing energy. However, medical associations continue to ignore the healing energy means of treatment.

Friendly guides and companions

46

PART 3—Love, kindness and prayer

First cancer patient

(Auckland, New Zealand)

There had been a black scab on my arm along with lots of other scars and scabs from damage during the winter working with a chain saw among very rough timber. When the doctor saw it he cut it out there and then and took out a piece as big as my thumb. There were also other spots on my neck, chest and forehead which he advised me to get removed later.

I called at another doctor one day to have them frozen off, but when he saw how much there was to do he said, "I haven't enough liquid nitrogen to do all that, you had better call in at the beginning of the month and I will have a new supply and I will do them all together."

I had just had some success with the healing of a little bird and was on the way to Te Kuiti to do some healing work with Peter. We were kept very busy for three days and were getting a lot of success with patients with every kind of ailment. We were using this healing energy continually for three days and I hadn't even thought of the spots on my neck and chest, but when I called at the doctor to get them removed we discovered they had all gone. Often the more you try to help others the more you receive back yourself.

On the way home that night my brother asked me to call and see a friend of his who had been sent home from the hospital to die of cancer. When I called to see him, he was just skin and bone and was a green yellow colour and couldn't keep down any food or liquid, had lost all control of his bowels and bladder and I was told there was just black muck and blood coming away from him. To look at him you wouldn't think he would last more than a few hours.

I could feel some cold areas in his aura and kept working over him until all the cold areas had gone and there was just a warm glow coming from his body filling the whole room. He said he felt wonderful, better than he had for months. The next morning I called in again to see if he was still alive and couldn't believe my eyes. He was sitting up in bed eating a meal. He had colour in his cheeks and had control of his bowels and bladder again.

I didn't see him again for many weeks, but heard he had been out digging in the garden and had fallen over and broken his leg. Weeks after that I went to see him in hospital and there was still no sign of the cancer.

Stories told as part of healing

(Springfield, Missouri)

At times during healing, or soon after, you may get an urge to tell a story that doesn't seem to relate to the person at the time, but later you will find you needed to tell that story for a reason.

In a church in Missouri there was a woman who had been in great pain for eight months and nothing would relieve it. At first during healing relief was very slow. Then when there was more relief there was the urge to tell her a story that didn't seem to relate to her.

This story was of a man who was dying of cancer in Canada. He was in great pain, his body was all swollen up and tight like a drum, he was covered in sweat and moaning with pain. His wife and daughter were in the room with him, so after the pain had been reduced I asked them to feel the warm glow coming from his body, and then asked them to raise their hands to feel the energy shining down on him. He was in a state when many say they feel as if they are floating. So I said I thought that was what it was like when you died, you felt that warm glow then floated away in it. Then the man became conscious and began to talk normally. They said it was the first time he had been like that for many months, he looked very peaceful and comfortable and had no pain at all.

The family were very grateful that all the pain had gone. Then I went home and left them to have their family talk. Five hours later I rang back to see how he was, and his son answered and said Dad has just died, but the family are so grateful he had those few hours without pain, and was able to sort out all the family problems they hadn't been able to discuss before, and was able to talk to the family normally for a few hours. Then he just shut his eyes and went to sleep like a baby, with all his family around him. They said the warm glow stayed with him after I left and they felt the presence of Jesus before he went. He looked so relaxed and peaceful that they were sure he had gone to a better place and they just couldn't be sad.

After this story the lady got up off the couch and said all the pain had gone. Then she danced to the door and showed her friends that there was no pain any more.

Later I learnt she had lost a son in an accident and couldn't accept the fact that he had gone, and that was when the pain had started. From the time she got up off the couch after treatment the pain did not re-occur. It did seem that she needed to hear that story, and little stories like that have helped many people even though I didn't know at the time why I was telling them, but it turned out they were part of the healing.

Amy

(Calgary, Alberta)

One of the early people who contacted me in Canada was a mother who brought her six year old daughter Amy, who was dying of Leukemia.

From the day she was born her parents were told she wouldn't live to go to school, because her lungs weren't developed properly; there was nothing that could be done for her. Every breath was a struggle and she could be heard all over the house with each breath. Then at five she developed leukemia and was put in the cancer clinic.

Her parents went to see her one day and she was swollen up and had a rash all over her body. The mother said, "You are killing this girl with drugs, she is a delicate child and cannot stand this." The mother was told, "Your child is going to die anyway, all you have to do is go home and prepare for a funeral, there is nothing that can be done to save her."

The parents decided they weren't going to let her die like that. They had to have a court case with the clinic to get permission to take her home to die. The only reason they got permission was because the doctors were sure nothing could be done to save her. The parents took her to many more specialists, but got the same answer each time.

They kept her alive for a few more months with love, kindness, natural food, visualisation and prayers until they came to me.

When she came in the mother said, "How much is this going to cost and how often do I have to bring her?" Something made me say, "It won't cost one cent and bring her every day until she is better." At this time I had no idea what her trouble was, but was sure something could be done to help her. When I asked about her breathing I was told she had been like that all her life. After the first healing of 30 minutes she was taken home and slept all night, the first time in her life.

After the second day the lumps in her neck from the leukemia were gone and after the third day she was breathing normally. She was due for a check up at the clinic in eight days so I gave her treatment until then. Before she was taken into the clinic the mother showed me a photo of drugs in a plastic bag that the hospital had sent her to give this sick little girl. There looked to be enough to kill a horse, but the mother never used any of them because she was sure they were already killing her. When she was examined they said there is no sign of leukemia now. The mother said, "Don't you think she is looking better." The doctor replied that she wouldn't look like that if it wasn't for all the drugs they had sent for her. The mother said, "But I have told you three times that I never gave her any." He said, "You must have given her some, she couldn't look like that otherwise." The mother wanted to talk to him, but it was just like talking to a computer that had been programmed to one thing only. On the medical reports it said it was the amount of drugs that were given to the girl after being sent home that brought about the cure. Everyone who had any contact with the family knew that it was only after the drugs were stopped that she started to recover.

When we came out of the hospital the mother said, "Can't we put a letter in the paper to say that children don't have to die due to side effects of drugs? That they can recover at home without them?" I said, "I have already had reporters from TV and the papers, but their stories weren't allowed to be made public." In the U.S.A. and Canada in those days for some reason nobody was allowed to mention anyone who had recovered from terminal illness.

However, the family got a phone call from Amsterdam a few days later from a lady who had also taken her daughter away from the cancer clinic there. She had heard about Amy's recovery and said she had a friend in Argentina, who had also taken her child away from a cancer clinic and that she would be getting in touch with Amy's mother to hear more about Amy.

This shows that the word of Amy's recovery had got around the world in a few days without the help of TV or newspapers. It seems that bad news is always in the headlines, but good news is communicated by word of mouth.

No time off

(Calgary, Canada)

After working seven days per week for over three years I was in the cancer clinic late one night and mentioned to the doctor that I would like to have my ear cleaned out some time when he wasn't busy. He said, "We will do it now." He tried one syringe, and when that didn't work he got another one and put a lot of pressure on it. The end came off the syringe and broke in my ear drum. The next day I was stone deaf and had a bad headache.

I thought to myself, if I had had one day a week off for the last three and a half years that would be over 150 days. Should I ask God for some time off to get some rest? Before I could ask, the answer came loud and clear, THERE IS TOO MUCH TO DO, WE CAN'T GIVE YOU ANY TIME OFF BUT IF YOU GET REALLY TIRED WE WILL LET YOU DIE 150 DAYS EARLIER.

I said, "It doesn't matter God, I am not really all that tired, I will carry on." If I had taken any time off I would never have got to Missouri the next week.

One step at a time—February 1990

(Springfield, Missouri)

Lake disaster and lesson to thousands

At the church Freddy told his story of one step at a time. His boat had sunk when he was out fishing with his best friend. Freddy had one lifejacket and couldn't swim. His friend was heading for shore when Freddy saw him go under and not come up again. He was left there alone in the bitter cold lake. He said, "I need your help God, I can't get out of here alone." A voice told him to struggle in a certain direction and there would be a broken branch of a tree there and he would be able to rest on that. Finding it, resting for a while and being nearly frozen, he said, "Look God there is a fishing line tangled all around my legs, how can I get away from here?" He was told to leave his boots and pants behind and to struggle for the shore. When he finally got to the shore there was just a lake in front of him and a mountain behind. He said, "What do I do now God, there is no help here and I will freeze to death tonight." He was told to stuff all his clothes with dry leaves to keep himself warm and dry and to make a bed of dry leaves.

He managed to stay alive all night and in the morning said, "What do I do now God?" He was told that over the top of the mountain there was a road and when he got to it he would find help. He tried to walk, but kept on falling over. He said, "Look God I can't even walk. How am I going to get to that road?" He was told, "You can crawl can't you." With frost bitten feet and hands it took him more than 10 hours to crawl over the mountain, and he thought he would die of thirst before he found help. When he finally got to the road there was a child's plastic toy broken and lying there full of rain water. Finally he crawled along the road to a house where he got help. His message was, "God will always guide you, but only one step at a time, and you have to do it yourself." He will always help but not always the way you expect him to. If your car is broken down on the road and you are walking home and you say, please God send along someone in a Cadillac to give me a ride, Freddy said help will come, but it may not be a Cadillac, it may be a mad grizzly bear coming down the road. Then you find your own legs can carry you home.

If I had had any time off I would never have heard that story. I have told it many times since and been thanked by many people. The first time was at a meeting of alcoholics and many people thanked me, saying they had been taught one day at a time, but had never known they had to do it all themselves and not to expect anyone to do it for them.

So many people have said they have had great benefit from hearing Freddy's story, which has changed hundreds of peoples lives, that I was glad I didn't have time off.

Working with a Russian healer

(Springfield, Missouri)

I had the privilege of attending a church in Missouri where a Russian visitor was giving the Sermon in English. There were people there from every nationality on a global peace walk, doing this stage across America. After this sermon while giving healing to a young girl with cerebral palsy, I was introduced to another Russian who was a healer and who couldn't speak a word of English.

She made signs to me that when the sun went down and came up again God, she and I would work on this girl for five hours. So we arranged to do that.

The girl had been in a wheelchair all her life and was 11 years old. Her whole body was stiff, with the joints in her hands, arms and legs almost locked in one position.

Two other people, who did massage, came to help. This Russian lady, who was also a doctor and chiropractor, made up her own lubrication for massage from the juice of an apple and lemon mixed with some honey. There was also something else which I don't remember, it may have been juice from an onion. She had to mix this herself from the fruit.

They first started on the joint of every finger, massaging and concentrating on loosening up every joint and muscle. I was just working above the body and drawing away the pain from where they were working. When they got down to her abdomen I could feel a hot pain coming from there and they showed me there was a painful lump there. When I signalled that I could feel pain coming from there through my hands, she put her hands towards heaven and was thanking God for his energy. When the pain started to become less she signalled to me it was feeling softer and smaller to them also. By the time the pain had gone the lump had also gone.

It seemed strange that I was drawn there from New Zealand and the woman drawn there from Russia. We couldn't speak a word of each other's language, but were both being guided by God to work on this girl in our own way and combining our efforts to help a girl, who happened to be there and needed help.

By the time five hours had passed the girl's whole body was relaxed and she could fold her arms behind her head, or behind her back and do things she had never been able to do before. When I carried her out to the car her whole body was just like a rag doll, there was no stiffness in her joints, it almost felt as if she had no bones in her body at all.

That night she stood up by herself, the first time in her life. A few days later she was walking with the help of a walker and she looked so radiant, as if the sun was shining out of her. The last I heard, she was improving all the time and the loving energy shining out of her was giving help to anyone who came in contact with her.

We definitely were guided to work together on this girl. We had the feeling this was happening in every country, with every nationality.

Hymns of thanks to God

(Springfield, Missouri)

While in Canada there was a phone call from Nancy Hoflund of Springfield, Missouri, asking for healing to be sent to five people who were not able to be helped by anything the medical science could do for them. She also said there were other people wanting help so I decided to fly down the next day and Norm Hoflund was there to meet me at the Airport. He then took me to his home to stay for a few days.

There were five people there when we arrived. The first thing they asked me was could I send healing to a young girl who was in hospital dying of cancer, there was nothing medical science could do for her to relieve the stress and pain she was going through.

We sent her healing prayers first then sent more to six or seven others before retiring for the night. We felt a lot of pain and stress come away from them all although we were many miles away from most of them. I didn't know at the time, but Chic Johnston a minister from the Unity church was one of the people present. He and his wife had been sitting up all night with the family and the young girl that was dying. She was in great pain and very upset about dying so young and it was upsetting the family and all the staff.

She was a beautiful girl with a beautiful voice and loved by everyone in the church. The first thing the minister said in church the next day was that when they went to see her that night after healing had been sent to her, she was sitting up in bed and said she had no more pain and had felt the presence of Jesus and knew he wanted her for a special reason. She knew she had to go and was going to a better place. She knew she would be happy there and she wanted all her family to come to see her because she wanted to explain that nobody was to be sad, she could feel the presence of Jesus and had no more pain and was ready to go, but wanted to say goodbye to everyone first. In the church that day the minister thanked God for sending me to Missouri to help them with their prayers. A few days later she died happy and peaceful with no pain.

Then the minister opened the church for healing for the ten days I was there. In that time there were seventy people came and some of them more than once.

The day before leaving Missouri, there were eight people in the basement of a private home, some for healing and others who were helping with the healing and getting experience. Occasionally others would come to join in. When Noah Karsh called in he had a friend with him. I asked if he wanted healing or to help us. He said he was just a friend of Noah's and wanted to watch.

Noah's friend just stood back very quietly until I started to pray aloud while healing, then he started to sing hymns very quietly. He had a beautiful voice which allowed you to feel vibrations go right through your body. He kept on singing and others slowly joined in. Nancy Hoflund and many others from upstairs also came down to join in until the place was full. He told us about when he was a boy living up in the Rockies where they could hear the train going through the mountains at night. There was a black train driver who used to play OH HOW I LOVE JESUS, OH HOW I LOVE JESUS, BECAUSE HE LOVED ME FIRST on the train whistle every night as he went through the mountains for everyone living in those mountains to hear. Then he gave a demonstration of what the train sounded like as it went through the mountains playing hymns on the train whistle. While he was giving this imitation of the hymn being played on the train whistle you could hear the whistle echoing through the mountains as the train disappeared in the distance. This man used to sing on TV and gave performances to large audiences all over U.S.A. and in other countries. Then for over two hours while we were healing one person after another he was leading everyone with hymns. It was the most wonderful experience I have ever had.

It was the most moving experience. There were tears of joy in the eyes of everyone there when the singing stopped and he left to go home. We got the message later that this wonderful singer was the father of the young girl who had died without any pain or distress and he had just come to give thanks to God and to thank us for our prayers but was so overwhelmed by the tears of joy of everyone present he was unable to speak when he left, so we didn't get the message until later.

Casey

(Boulder, Colorado)

While in Colorado I was asked if I would go to see a five year old boy named Casey who was dying of Leukemia. I didn't know that the parents had been told that the boy only had about two hours to live, also I didn't know they had another healer there the same day. Casey just screamed and wouldn't let the other healer near him in any way, so I don't know how they decided to let me see him.

They told me about the other healer being there, so I sat well away from him and just let the energy flow through me from a distance. In a few minutes Casey was more relaxed and I was able to sit close to him. In a bit over half an hour he was free of pain and was playing with his little brother around the room, but in a short time the pain would come back and he would have to lie down again. So I knew it would be necessary to stay with him all night. During the night he would get pains again and I would

Casey Thornton at his special place overlooking Boulder, Colorado

tell him God was allowing the pain to come away from him through my hand. Then he would relax and go to sleep again. After staying up with him all that night and seven more nights it was necessary for me to go back to Missouri. I didn't know how I could possibly go and leave him. When the plane took off I realised part of me had stayed with him. All night I would have to get up every two hours to send him healing. Then one morning there was a great peace and I knew he had either recovered or gone. His mother rang me soon after to say he had gone peacefully.

Before I met him Casey had had a bone marrow transplant and almost died. He told his parents he had only come back from the other side to tell them he didn't want them to be sad, because he had been there and knew he had to go back for a special reason, but wanted to tell his parents and friends not to be sad. He said it was beautiful there and everyone loved you and the light was so bright but it didn't hurt your eyes. His mother asked, "Did you see God when you saw the white light?" He said, "Mum, God is the white light."

He had asked his three year old brother if he knew anything about death. His brother said, "I only know my little insect died and can't breathe any more." Casey said, "No, he can't breathe any more, but that is only a part of him—the part he doesn't need any more. The main part is still alive dancing with God." Casey said, "I am going to be like that. I won't be able to grow up with you. God wants me for a special reason and I have to go away. You will be able to play with all the toys yourself because I won't be here." After talking to his little brother he said to his father, "Now is the time for us to go to our special place," and they went away on the motor bike up to a big rock in the mountains where they could look out all over Colorado.

A few days later he went to the school to talk to all his friends and answer any questions. He told the children the same as he had told his mother and father: that everyone loved you there. They asked was he going to come back. He said he thought so, but didn't know when. They asked about all his toys, clothes and things. A few nights before he died he said to his mother, "I want you to promise to have another baby because I want to come back and I want to come back with you." His mother said, "It takes two to make a baby", and he said "Dad will have to promise too." Both parents promised, then he said, "I don't care if I come back as a girl, because actually girls did have it better than boys because they could get all dressed up in pretty clothes."

I received letters from Casey's mother and father and also one from a family friend, who lived in Texas. They testified as to how well Casey felt after receiving healing energy and recounted Casey's wish that his story be told about the loving reality he sensed during his after death experience to help remove people's fear about dying and death. Casey used to talk so much with his mother and friends of death that we all realised that our life on earth was a very small part of our existence. At the funeral the mother and father were the only ones who weren't upset. They were happy because to them the main part of Casey was still alive and part of him was still with them and always would be. "Part of him will always be with me also," the father spoke in church, and thanked God for the privilege of having Casey for as long as they did. Casey was on TV a lot and changed thousands of people's lives just by seeing him. I also thank God for the privilege of those few days shared with him and part of him will always be with me also.

Our son, Casey, had only hours to live after a 2 year long struggle with leukemia. His white blood count was 195,000, more than 20 times normal, and all systems in his body were ceasing to function. Rod Campbell came, like an angel, to help him. Now, four days later, the physicians involved in the case are amazed—not only that Casey is still alive, but that there has been marked improvement in every way both physically and emotionally. Casey's will to live is beginning to appear—and we believe full healing is in store for an otherwise "terminal" child. We thank you, bless you, and love you dearly, Rod! Your gift of healing is phenomenal—and what you have to show with all people is beyond words! Thank you for being in our lives! Our love to you!

Julie Thornton & Family.

There was also a letter from Casey's father a few weeks later, which said that from the time we met Casey had no more need for drugs to relieve pain.

Although the doctors couldn't believe the improvement in his condition, Casey and the family knew that God wanted him for a special purpose. They were so grateful that he had those extra days with them and his friends completely without pain.

During this period they were able to discuss freely the experiences he had been through and the fact that Casey didn't want anybody to be sad when he had to go, and the fact that he wanted to come back some day and hoped he could come back to them. In many ways he was ready to go because he said it was so wonderful there where everybody loved you so much, and the light was so beautiful, but didn't hurt your eyes.

The parents wanted me to be present when their new baby arrived two years later, but unfortunately the delays with immigration officials had prevented me from being there at that time.

We don't have to give up on people just because the medical association says there is nothing medical science can do for them. First we have to give them love, kindness and prayers and ask that they be comfortable and happy until they have to go and in so many cases their change of attitude at this time will be a new beginning for them. This is when they start appreciating the little things in nature and keep on doing that for many years.

Casey was only five years old, but so many lives have been changed by the fact that he came back from the other side and shared his experiences with so many. The ripples from the number of people's hearts he touched while he was here will be going around the world for many years to come.

The white light

(Boulder, Colorado)

In Boulder, Colorado we had an evening together with approximately 30 nurses and a few doctors.

I had never told anyone that while healing my mind is always on the fact that the healing energy is coming from above, and going through my hands. There is no physical feeling in me and it feels at times as if my physical body is not there at all.

While giving healing to a patient, there were five of the nurses who were helping and telling us of the experiences that they were feeling. Some could feel everything the same as I could and actually felt the different types of pain in different parts of the body.

Two of the nurses who were there could see auras, one sitting on each side of the room. When we had finished they were saying what they had seen. While we were healing they sometimes saw other spirits around us, then a white light came down through the ceiling and gradually surrounded us all at the table. Then when things were quiet the light got so dense around me they were unable to see me.

In Missouri there was a girl who used to sing in front of the people present and always had tears running down her cheeks. When she was singing you could feel vibrations of energy going up and down your body. There was a different vibration in the church while she sang. When I told her what these people had seen she said, "That is what I see when I am singing. First there is a white light coming down over one or two people then gradually it slowly comes down over everyone until I can't see anyone in the church, but as soon as the minister starts to talk, it all lifts and goes away."

At times it seemed to me as if there was a figure standing above and behind me in a white light with arms outstretched. I had never told anyone about this before. A priest in Canada asked me to go with him to help where they were giving healing to a little boy with leukemia. There were six nuns present and we were all working in the room with a few around the boy and others just praying, but some of the nuns sitting back could see a figure standing behind us with his arms out-stretched.

Phantom pain

(Springfield, Missouri)

One thing worth mentioning is that in my travels I have often been asked to give healing to people with phantom pains.

All the pain can be felt there, just as it was before the limb was taken away. So it seems as if it would be reasonable to say that the diseases were probably formed in the aureole or spiritual body before they were developed in the physical body. At times it is possible to describe exactly what the pain is like in the limb that was removed. When the pain is removed from the phantom limb, it will disappear from the person. Often when pain has been removed from a phantom limb, soon after an operation, the doctors are amazed at how quickly the wound has healed. To just remove a diseased limb from a body is not the complete answer because the disease is still in close contact with the body and can still cause trouble or spread.

The healer's hands will float over a person's body then stop above where there is any trouble. There were many times when an assistant would come into a room where there was a man with a wooden leg, but the assistant didn't know about it. In every case their hands would go above the wooden leg and they would feel the trouble that had been there, but after removing the trouble their hands wouldn't go back there any more.

In another case in Missouri there was a woman with great pain in her arm which had been removed many months before. The healer could feel a great pressure that was throbbing and a burning pain in that arm. The lady said that was exactly what she felt, but after two treatments the pain had gone.

Loss of weight and visualisation

(Calgary, Alberta)

A person came to me with a bad hip and with pain right in the bone. She was also twice what should have been her normal weight. For three or four times I worked on that hip every second day and the pain was almost gone. Then when she came in after a weekend and climbed onto the table there were big bulges down on one side of her body and there were just gentle curves on the side that had been worked on for the hip pain. So it was necessary to work on her all over to get her even on both sides. After a few weeks she was even on both sides and had lost eight inches around her hips. She was very happy because the pain as well as the weight had gone. So although the original problem was hip pain the treatment also reduced her weight. To reduce the weight all over the body it became necessary to treat the whole person and not just the hip. The lady was over-joyed at the result having two of her problems cured when she sought a treatment for just one.

There was another lady who came in who was three times her normal size from the waist down. Her legs were black and blue from where blood vessels had burst. She had no knees or ankles. Her legs were the same shape from the hips to the feet. Her blood pressure was so high she was on the danger list all the time and had been told that medical science couldn't do anything to help her. She came twice and everything went back to normal and the blood pressure was normal after one day.

Two other ladies who were both close to three hundred pounds wanted to come every day for five days to lose weight. I had told them to use visualisation all the time and visualise themselves running and jumping or dancing every time they heard music. They did this and had healing treatment as well. After three days there was a change. The younger one was still going to University. The elder one said her sister spends all her time fighting off the boys now and the younger one added, "Well actually, I don't fight too hard."

Another lady, who had been an Olympic discus thrower, had put on a lot of weight when she retired and she used visualisation only for three weeks. When I saw her again she looked totally different. She had not lost so much weight, but had a big change in her shape. All the soft flesh had gone. I am sure visualisation can help in the cure of all ailments and I do think it is of great benefit in keeping the body healthy.

Crawling

(Calgary, Alberta)

In Canada I was taken to a person who had a child who had brain damage and was 16 months old and had never shown any signs of wanting to crawl or move. They had been to the best specialists in the world and just that day had the final answer which said that the child would never recover and would never walk. Also, that it would always be brain damaged and would never improve, but would get worse.

She took me home to see the boy, and he was just lying still. So the mother held the child in her arms and I explained to her that when possible I was guided to let the healing energy go through the mother into the child with wonderful results. It felt to me as if some of the mother's energy in her immune system would go into the baby with her love and respect for the baby.

Within minutes the mother said, "He looks different," and she could feel a difference in him. His colour had definitely changed and there was a warm glow shining out of the baby. The mother was very excited about the change and wanted to bring him to me the next day. We arranged for her to be there at two o'clock. She said she was a member of the Crippled Children's Association and would bring another lady with her baby who was the same.

The next day at two o'clock there was no sign of her and after a long wait I rang the house and the girl who looks after children said, "She left here to go to you at twenty to two. She should be there by now." She never came or contacted me and went away to Germany for 10 days the next morning. When she returned the baby was crawling all over the house. I saw him a few more times and he was walking and riding his horse. When he was just learning to walk I was there one day and wanted to pick him up to give him a hug, but he was crawling very fast to get away from me under the chairs and table. Then when I kept after him he rushed over to his toy box and got his gun to stop me. So I knew there was nothing wrong with his brain.

The mother did not mention why she had not turned up that day with the other child. This has happened before when people have been uncertain and have talked to ministers about it and many of them will say that any healing done outside their church must be the work of the devil and will advise people against it. I believe that is what the churches teach them to say. However, other ministers and priests will come and see for themselves that we are only using love, kindness and respect. They will also bring members of their own families and take me to people they are unable to help themselves. Then with our combined efforts we are able to get results.

The gift of healing was shown to help a little bird in trouble and all living things, no matter what race or religion or species of life, for no recognition or reward. So I can't say I will only give healing in any one church.

I wondered what could be done about this and talked about it to someone. One man said, "Well how do you think Christ would get on if he came back today?" This gave me a lot to think about and made me realise I was much happier working with people with no money, out in an Indian Reservation or in the mountains with nature and this is where I like to work better than anywhere else. Not in a huge expensive church where all I can feel is the amount of money that people have spent on building that church.

The nicest church I have been taken to was supposed to be the first church built in Canada in the Calgary area not far from Okatokes. It was built of logs, which were cut up in the mountains, by a man wanting to build a ranch house. He cut them all himself and floated them down the river to where they were needed and on the last day he was accidentally drowned. He had no relations so the ranchers decided to use the logs to build a church. Ranchers had just finished reblocking it and doing some repairs when they took me to see it.

I tried to walk right down the aisle, but the energy made me stop half way down. I could feel all the love, sweat and tears, joy and sadness that had been experienced in that church over all those years. I was also able to feel how much it had meant to those early settlers, who must have travelled for days by buggy to attend. This church was built of natural materials, of logs standing side by side and cracks filled with clay and horsehair. All labour was done with love by volunteers. They didn't need to ask for money from people who were in need. The people who were capable gave their services free.

I was invited there one day to attend a Thanksgiving service. Settlers were there from hundreds of miles around and in the church were old implements used by the first settlers. There were also cages with every kind of pet imaginable whose ancestors had shared those hard times with the settlers.

Every time the minister hesitated in his sermon there would be a few words from a bird or animal. All the way through the service they were joining in and made everyone, not only feel close to Jesus, but part of nature itself, sharing with all living things and giving thanks to God for the privilege of being there. They were also thanking God for the privilege of being able to share that experience with the descendants of all those people who built the church and to be able to share it with the descendants of the animals and birds that were there at the time. Although a lot of sadness could be felt there, there was more love and respect than I have ever felt in any church, before or since.

Debra

(Calgary, Alberta)

One night during a blizzard in Canada a lady came to me who helped me to learn a lot.

She had noises in her ears and all sorts of problems and had been abused as a child. She couldn't trust anyone and everyone she had any faith in had let her down. She was a small attractive person and very cold when she arrived.

She reminded me of a cold, hungry, frightened little animal anyone would love to hold in their arms and give love and comfort to. She had been let down so often she just could not relax or let anyone show any affection towards her. Although we used to try, there was no way she would relax enough for the healing to be of benefit. She would start to relax, but as soon as she felt the warmth and comfort coming from the healing she would just tighten up again. It seemed hopeless, but thank God she did keep coming back time after time.

It had been my method of working on a person until there was a warm glow coming from them and I could feel it like a bubble of healing energy around their body and they would feel a warm glow all through. This afternoon the warm glow was just building up when it felt as if my hands were being pushed away from her. They were already about 14 inches away, but were being pushed further back so I shifted further and further back from her and by raising my hands with the palms upwards could feel this warm glow was shining down on her from above. Her whole expression had changed and she was completely relaxed, her eyes were looking up through the ceiling and she didn't seem aware that I was there.

This made me realise she was now getting the love and comfort she so badly needed from the proper place. Before that she said she had never ever felt any closeness to God or felt anything in a church. From then on she was a different person. She was able to relax completely and we were able to work on one of her problems at a time until she had confidence in herself and went ahead and could do anything she chose to do.

From then on I've always known that the warm glow that people feel in their bodies and that I can feel around them is really shining down on them from above and they are getting the love, comfort and healing energy from the right place. There was no need for me to do anything myself, but just guide the energy to go through my hands to where it was needed and keep back to let the other energy shine down from above.

Visualisation to a girl who was in a coma

(Calgary, Alberta)

This is a story I must tell you about a 12 year old child who had been in a car accident and was in a coma. They didn't think she would come out of it. A lady who was working with me heard about it and, as she was living alone, she used to send her healing every night and visualise herself going up to the girl's room and talking to her. She kept doing this every night for many weeks. Although she had never met the girl she finally got her to open her eyes and then was saying, "You have to start moving now", but the girl used to say, "I can't I am too tired, I just can't move." So she was told to concentrate on one toe and work on that every day then gradually work on the other parts of her body.

After many weeks the girl was able to move, then walk and finally did get out of hospital. Then six months later this lady was at church one day and a young girl came running up to her crying and said, "I have been looking for you everywhere," and the lady said, "But I don't know you, do I?" The girl replied, "Yes, you do, you used to come and see me in Hospital." The girl had told the doctors and family, but they said you must not say things like that—it never happened. The mother called the girl away while they were talking and wouldn't let them talk together again. Even though they had never met, this young girl recognised the lady who had been sending her healing.

While in Canada there was a phone call from New Zealand to say there was a girl in hospital with two brain tumours. She was in a lot of pain and they rang to ask if we could do anything to give her relief from the pain. They never asked for any cure. This was the 17th of December at 2.30 AM and she was supposed to die before Christmas. I gave her absentee healing straight away and I could feel the two tumours, a short one and one much longer. I could also feel the throbbing pain coming from them. I could feel the tumours in my hand and threw them out the window. Then there was a warm glow coming from the body and no sign of any pain. Next morning they rang me again to say in the night all the pain had gone and she was sitting up in bed eating a meal and was going home for Christmas. Weeks later they rang again and said she had been to three cancer clinics and they could find no sign of tumours and could not understand how they had made a mistake. That is over three years ago and she is still well.

It seems ridiculous or impossible to say this happened, but when you think that with prayers, you are just tapping into energy from God, which created all living things and the whole universe. So what we use of that energy is nothing at all. Distance and time are no problem. If we can stop and remove one tumour from ten thousand miles away, why not two, or why not ten? If we could use our combined efforts, we have no idea what we could do to help others, or all living things.

Healing prayers for Dick requested from New Zealand

(Seattle, Washington)

I received a message from New Zealand telling me that a man from there had been flown to Saint Joseph's Hospital in Washington, U.S.A. Since the doctors at St Joseph's had done all they could, Dick had been taken off all life support systems, drugs and food and was considered brain dead.

He had been put in a side room to die and was only expected to live for a few hours.

Two weeks before I ever heard of this man, I was in Edmonton visiting when a man I had met, John Roberts, asked me to come to his house. He wanted me to meet his wife who had been suffering terrific pain for many years. After we had given her healing prayer he discovered he could feel her pain coming out of her body through his hands. He could also feel the love and healing power coming directly from Jesus into her body. He gave me a meal and a cheque before I left. I didn't look at the cheque at the time, but when I returned to Calgary I discovered that he had given me $500.00. This turned out to be exactly the amount of money I needed for a plane ticket to Washington State to see Dick two weeks later!

The family who had called from New Zealand knew of me and asked me to give Dick some healing. At home in Calgary at 2.00 AM in the morning I was giving Dick absentee healing when a branch broke off a tree just outside my window during a rain storm. The light shining from the park into the window made the shape of a perfect cross in the middle of the room with three or four smaller crosses below it. As my hands moved over the spiritual body of Dick to remove all pain and pressure the wind outside my window made the cross sway back and forth in time with the movement of my hands. There was a terrific amount of pressure and pain coming from Dick's head and in the blood stream down as far as his chest. There was also pressure in the blood stream in his legs. From then on every time I did absentee healing for him there was a big improvement in his body condition. Although I could feel a big improvement in body condition I did not think it would be visible.

The next day I gave more healing and then flew to Washington to see Dick. I arrived in the late afternoon and stayed up all night with Dick and gave him healing until 7.30 in the morning. I stayed up for 27 hours and was not a bit tired. Dick was definitely improving and the family began making preparations to return to New Zealand. Dick's body felt the same to me as his spiritual body had felt hundreds of miles away. While sitting with Dick I often thought of Sister Mary Christopher and others who had sat with me all night when I was sick in the Mater Hospital in New Zealand. I thanked God that I was able to give back some of that kindness to others and feel that the kindness given to me was not wasted.

The reaction of the hospital staff was amazing. This patient, who had been put in a side room to die overnight, then brought back into the ward in the morning with his blood pressure and temperature back to normal, and with no pain, seemed to have a very special place in the hearts of the whole staff. He was lying there so peacefully with such good colour in his cheeks.

The nurses coming on duty used to come into his room every morning and when they were with him there were tears of joy in their eyes and some would be crying and hugging each other in the corridor before going to work. In the evening others would call in with the same reaction.

An insurance company sent a doctor and a nurse from Australia to be with him on the plane back to New Zealand. So there were doctors and nurses from Canada, Australia, U.S.A. and New Zealand all interested in the change in his condition.

His eyes were open and he knew what was going on around him. The day he left there was a nurse who came in to see him who was able to communicate with him. She had lost a husband with a brain haemorrhage and she used to tell him to shut his eyes twice for yes and once for no. This worked well, but it was only for a few minutes. As it was just before he left I didn't get a chance to talk to the family about it. One reason was I felt sure he would just go ahead when he got back to New Zealand. Unfortunately the medical association in New Zealand didn't have the same interest in him as the doctors and staff did in U.S.A.

One Sister said to me it was a great spiritual experience for the family and for the whole staff at the hospital. After the first night at the hospital I was able to get four hours rest, then sat up with him all night checking his condition every hour until he was flown back to New Zealand. This was another 21 hours and I still didn't feel one bit tired or hungry. I only thought about food when some of the family would bring something to eat or drink.

It seems that when you are working close to nature, you are also working close to God, and while giving healing prayers you are also getting energy yourself at the same time. While working with stock close to nature, in my younger days, many people used to ask me how I could work all day and never feel hungry. While doing this work close to nature and working always by instinct or being guided there was no feeling of hunger, but doing any other type of work a bit to eat or a drink of tea was very welcome every two hours. We do seem to get extra energy ourselves while trying to help other living things and working close to nature.

Leaving Missouri

(Springfield, Missouri)

The first time I went to Missouri I had 70 patients come to me in two weeks. They all gave good donations and I thought that would be a place to make my headquarters. So when I went back two months later (some doctors and some churches had asked me to come) I booked an apartment for six weeks. Once I arrived there, many doctors and many people from churches said they would send people, but hardly anyone came. Something always happened at the last minute and they couldn't make it. The people who did come were very bad cancer patients and they had no money. I wouldn't accept any money from them so my income was practically cut off.

I stopped there for over a month and my money was getting less and less. One lady who used to come with very bad cancer insisted that I take $2 and some days that was all the income I had. There was a restaurant down the road where you could have all you could eat for $6. If you only had dessert you could have all you could eat for 70 cents. There was apple pie, fruit salad, as much ice cream as you wanted, almost anything you could think of. So I used to live on desserts in those lean days.

But then the people from the churches and doctors who came to see me said, "There's something wrong, why aren't people coming? We should have advertised in the paper or over the air." I said, "No, if people are supposed to be here they would be here. I didn't advertise when I first went to Canada and everyone was there waiting. I feel God wants me to go in a different direction."

So while I didn't have much to do, my time was spent writing to the doctors I had met who were keen to use more alternative treatments and natural foods, with less chemicals and drugs. The Medical Association rules prevented them from doing this at that time. They were not happy with the rules and had said, "What can we do on our own? We want to keep our jobs and our licences." I suggested they have a newsletter between them all, so they could keep in touch with each other to share their problems. So I was doing a lot of correspondence with people, but then I decided that if I couldn't make enough to live on I'd have to leave here. Once I'd made up my mind to leave I decided to go back to Canada to pick up the rest of my gear and go back to New Zealand.

The day before I left there were four young people who had got in contact with me and had come for healing. We were all going to meet at a church and I was going to introduce them to each other. I was really disappointed that I hadn't come in contact with children who needed help. This upset me a bit. I went to the church this day. There were four young people and they were all so excited to meet each other because they all definitely had gifts of healing and wanted to spend their lives helping others.

They were that thrilled and excited about meeting each other that they were talking and talking among themselves, so pleased to be in a group they almost forgot that I was there. It made me realise I don't have to do the healing, I just had to bring these people together and they could do the healing. That made me realise that was the direction I had to take, and I decided that at the church.

I went home from the church and I was supposed to pack everything ready to leave by bus for Calgary, Alberta at 5.00 AM the following morning. Instead two of these young people ran me back to the church and wanted me to tell them all I could about healing and do all I could before I went.

I hadn't been there long before someone came in wanting healing, so I said, "You'd better come and work with me to see what you can feel as we work together." So they came in and they could feel everything I could feel.

They were going away to India in a few days so they wanted to do all they could before they went. That person was finished and she gave me a donation and then just as I was thinking about starting to pack, two more people came in and they both wanted healing and wanted to know if I could possibly give them some before I left. They also each gave me donations. Then others came and they kept on coming till after 12 o'clock that night and I hadn't even started packing.

Once I started changing direction in doing what God wanted me to do and concentrate on drawing people together and getting other people started then money started flowing in again.

After these people left at 12.30 AM I had to start thinking about packing. I had to catch the bus at 5 o'clock in the morning so I didn't get much sleep that night. I finally got on the bus at five when the sun was just rising.

I saw the sun rise and set three times before arriving in Canada on the same bus. On the way to Canada, after passing through West Missouri we reached Idaho where we came to a crop of corn. It was a good crop with very dark leaves which showed there must be good soil below it. There were patches of sunflower among the corn and I got my camera out to take some photos to show my wife what the farming was like there. It was flat land as far as you could see in every direction. I thought as soon as we come to a different type of farming I would take some more photos, but we just went on and on with nothing to see but corn. Occasionally we would come to a small rise and as far as you could see in every direction there was nothing but corn. We travelled for 19 hours and there wasn't any change—just nothing but corn. That crop must have been almost as big as all New Zealand.

There was a man on the bus who was in terrible pain, so when we stopped for a few minutes for a cup of tea I asked him to put his leg up on a chair and I was able to take some of the terrible pain away. He said it was getting easier. He sat beside me in the bus and I was able to take more pain away from the leg from time to time.

He had been working at a cement factory and had gotten an infection in the bone from some chemicals. He had been to a doctor who had scraped the bone, which had relieved it and it was almost better when he got another infection. He didn't have enough money to go to the doctor to get it done again as it costs thousands of dollars over there, so he opened it up with a pocket knife and scraped the bone himself with no disinfectant, anaesthetic or antibiotics. You can imagine the pain he was in. Twice a day he would ask to have the pain removed and then other people in the bus would take turns in coming to sit by me for healing for one reason or another. So I was kept busy for the three days and nights of the journey. For three days and nights we were travelling all the time with just five minute breaks for a cup of tea every few hundred miles of the journey.

I was on my way to Calgary to pack all my gear to go back to New Zealand. In Calgary there were two letters waiting for me, one from Yukon and one from Alaska, asking me to go up there to hold a workshop and do healing. I rang and told them I would go up if they could find enough money to pay my expenses. They said they would pay for the plane tickets and make all arrangements. I stayed with a very nice family there and they had made arrangements for me to have a workshop in a church and then do healing in the same church. I was booked up with work from 9 o'clock in the morning until 11 o'clock at night. It was just non stop for 10 days.

They had arranged for people to make a donation to attend the workshop and for anyone wanting healing to make an extra donation. There was no time for rest at all and when I was leaving they gave me a huge handful of money. When I said you have to take the expenses out of that they said they already had. So I received enough money all the time I was there just because I changed my direction and was doing what God meant me to do—to draw these people together and make them realise they were to do the healing themselves. I just had to convince them that they could do it and it did work. In Alaska and Yukon there were a lot of people with Eskimo and Indian blood and they used to sing a chant that the Indians used while healing. It was beautiful and seemed to strengthen the healing energy that was coming through our hands.

74

"A bona fide healer"

(Calgary, Alberta)

This letter provides an example of what people felt had happened as a result of healing energy when I was in Canada:

April 24, 1988

To Whom it May Concern:

When I met Rod Campbell in early September, 1987, I was told by relatives and friends that I looked like death. I was listless and very pale, ashen. The doctors and the Tom Baker Cancer Centre in Calgary had just suspended my chemotherapy and Interferon treatments because they weren't working. On April 16, 1986 I was operated upon and found to have cancer of the right kidney and the cancer was too far advanced to be removed. They told me that I could possibly have a year to live. I was told that some types of treatment could be tried, but that the hoped-for success rate wasn't very high. They were right—the treatments didn't work.

By August 1987, the doctor at the Cancer Clinic told me there was nothing more they could do for me, gave me a prescription for a pain-killer and sent me home to die. At this point I had lost about 70 pounds and all hope seemed to be lost.

Through a friend I learned that a man named Rod Campbell had been doing amazing things to help people like myself. I decided it was worth a try and went to see him. After just two treatments I was up and walking around and eating better. Mr. Campbell doesn't claim to have any powers of his own, but rather is only a conduit for the Healing Power of God. During the next check-up at the cancer clinic I was told that the cancer was amazingly in remission and that the doctor couldn't believe that it was. Then I told him what I had been doing, he looked sceptical, but said, "Go for it." It has been seven months since that appointment and the doctor and nurses no longer look sceptical. They always ask about Mr. Campbell now and are intensely interested in my progress. The nurses call me, "Mr. Amazing Man", and the doctor tells me that by all known facts I shouldn't be walking around. For a man who didn't expect to see his 47th birthday I am now looking forward to my 48th in 4 more days.

In my opinion, it is Rod Campbell and not me who is, "Mr. Amazing Man." I thank God he was put in my path when I needed him most.

Many people I have met since feel the same way that I do. I have seen what Mr. Campbell has done and is doing for so many people that I am convinced he is a bona fide healer. We need more people like him in this country. His only sermon has been that with love and kindness and the power of God anyone can be cured.

Barry A. Deeves.

P.S. I am Elayne Deeves, Barry's wife, and I can attest to everything my husband has stated. I am a born sceptic, but there is no denying that Mr. Campbell has been a great asset to the lives of so many people. He is greatly needed here.

Elayne E. Deeves

PART 4—"And better things shall ye do"

Here I would like to refer to the story outlined earlier where a young woman who had two brain tumours was being prayed for by her family and friends. When she slipped into a coma with no expectation of recovery I received a call from New Zealand to help. Early next morning she was out of the coma and eating breakfast. Subsequent tests showed no brain tumours. Four years later this young lady has three healthy children with no sign of recurrence of the brain tumours. If one man in Canada can help channel God's healing energy to a young woman in the disappearance of two brain tumours, how much more could be done with many such people operating as channels of God's healing energy?

In order to help others to realise they have this ability I have set out in this part of the book an explanation of my experience when moved to help others.

Explaining what I feel

I am writing this to explain the feelings I have while giving healing and what I feel coming through my hands from the patient. I want to explain that this is what I was guided to do. I want to get this written down so that people who want to help others and can feel pain or stress from another person, will know how I was guided to start.

We all start off the same way with the same feelings because we have an overwhelming feeling of wanting to help someone with love, healing and prayers. At this moment this urge to help is more important than anything else in our lives.

We are willing to do anything to help people. At times, we even want to change places with the patients, we are so anxious to help them in any way. Open up completely and let the healing energy flow through you. This can only happen when your mind is fixed on the fact that the energy is coming from God.

When your heart and your mind are open to God and the patient and you feel the connection between the two, the energy does flow through you and you are just part of nature.

This cannot be done if there is anything else in your mind at all. Heartfelt prayer will assist the healer and the patient to attain the right frame of mind to succeed with the healing, but repeating prayers you have learnt may stop it, because part of your mind is on the book or the person you learnt from.

You will feel as if your physical body is not present. You do not have any physical feelings and you feel as if your physical body is not even there. Healing energy is going in through the right hand and any pain and discomfort is being drawn out with the left. That is how it feels when you relax completely and let the healing power flow through you. You are not aware of anything else. While doing that you should always visualise the patient as fit and well and never think of the patient as being sick or handicapped in any way.

I never wanted to feel pain, but that gift was given to me for some reason. That reason seemed to be to convince the doctors that this healing is real. When I went to Canada, doctors would bring patients to me and wouldn't tell me anything and I would be able to tell them what I could find. I could tell them what and where the pain was and whether it was nerve, muscle or bone pain or in the bloodstream. They always said I was 100% right.

As the healing developed, it was almost as if I was seeing with my hands because what I felt in the person's body I could see, not with my eyes, but in my mind. It was just as plain as if it was in front of my eyes.

A patient in Canada had pains in the abdomen and was diagnosed as having cancer and told she would need an operation and could never have children. When I put my hands above that area, I could only feel pain, swelling and tightness in the tubes from the ovaries. When I felt them, it was as if I could almost see those tubes all swollen and inflamed. I worked on her twice a week for about six weeks and the pain gradually reduced. She refused to have the operation and soon thereafter she became pregnant, but unfortunately lost the baby. Then I had to come back to New Zealand for a few weeks. When I returned to Canada and worked with her she became pregnant and said, "You can't go back to New Zealand until it is born." So I stayed in Canada for Christmas that year. She has had another child since and sends me many photos of the whole family.

When a person had a bleeding ulcer, the two fingers above the ulcer felt all raw as if all the skin had been taken off and the blood was dripping from them like a raw cut. After about 10 minutes, the wound healed up and the pain stopped. We have had some people with open ulcers on the legs and you could see the skin form over the ulcer and the redness go away within a few minutes as we were working on them. At times you can feel all sorts of pains in the body.

With cancer patients there is a lot of pain coming from the area where the cancer is, which can be felt with the left hand. After 3 or 4 days' treatment there is no pain coming from there at all, just numbness. If the doctors keep them on cortisone, they develop another pain which is just like a poison pain. The doctor in the cancer clinic said that it would be, because all treatment for cancer is poison. When the hands are put near the patient it just feels like wasp stings all over the hand, just like they were poisoned, hot and cold pain coming and throbbing. You have to keep on taking the pain away every day.

You feel many different sorts of pain all over the body. Sometimes you get a patient and you don't feel pain in the body, but if you reach your hand out 3 feet or more above the body and move it back and forth you may come to a layer of pain in the spiritual body. Above that there is none, below that there is none, only in one level in the spiritual body.

Then pray and ask that anything that is not of God and love be released. If the pain is still there, then ask everything from the past, no matter how far back, to be released. If the pain is still not released, then ask for any effects from drugs or chemicals to be released. If the pain persists ask for any effects from other people or taken on from other people to be released. Then the pain may drift away. Continue on about financial troubles, and continue until the pain leaves. When you hit the right thing the pain will leave.

Three times I had patients who were told they had a disease in the spinal cord and said nothing could be done for them. This disease would go right up the spinal cord and into the brain. They came to me and I could feel the terrific pain pumping out about 3 feet away on a certain level in the spiritual body. I asked anything not of God and of love to be taken away and the pain was removed before I even began healing. The patient was then able to get up off the table and touch his toes and the pain was gone. The patient couldn't feel any physical pain and I couldn't feel any from the physical body or the spiritual. Years later this pain was still not there.

It wasn't until I began writing this down that I realised that the pain from a certain level in the spiritual body is different from the pain in the physical body. You do not feel any nerve pain, muscle pain, bone pain, etc.; there is just pain. I did not realise there was such a difference. However, with a phantom pain from a limb that has been removed, the pain is exactly the same in the spiritual body as from the physical body.

Bone pain is easy to feel because you feel it in the bone in the hand, an achy, dull pain inside which can not be mistaken for anything else. The pain for blood pressure is different. Hold your left hand above the chest high above the body and move your right hand above the legs and up to the heart. You can feel the circulation in the area that you are moving over and you can tell where the blood is moving freely or where it is not. Or you can do it another way by moving your right fingers slowly over the person's body while having your left hand on the person's feet. You can then feel the person's condition and circulation in the left hand near the feet until it gradually improves. In other words from the left hand near the feet you can feel the condition of the circulation directly below the right hand wherever it is. The right hand scans the body while the left registers the condition.

In Canada one doctor came to me with no circulation in one leg and a large lump halfway between the knee and the ankle. There was no aura around the leg at all. He had been to many specialists, some in other countries. After I worked on him, some circulation came back and there seemed to be a large block where it was tight and hard for the blood to get through. As I worked it gradually lessened. Then the small blood vessels began to open and there were sharp little pains in my hand and I could feel them opening. Soon, blood was flowing freely. The next morning the doctor called me and the lump on his leg had also gone.

To feel these things, you must really be wanting to help the person with everything you've got. You must keep your mind on the fact that the energy is coming from God, not yourself. To keep myself reminded of this fact, I often pray to myself, although I also pray aloud so that the patient can also focus on this fact. Also, often the patient feels praying is important in the healing.

As I work on the body, the patient is usually very relaxed and almost feels as if he/she is floating.

Absentee Healing

Giving Absentee healing it is just the same as praying for a person who is not present in their physical form. But when you ask to be able to feel all the pain in that person's body it is possible to feel all the pain and the condition of the person as if they were right there with you.

It is all done through prayer and with God's permission, because you first ask God for permission to be able to feel the pain in that person's body.

While doing this you don't have any physical feelings yourself, so you cannot be sure if the other person's spiritual body is extended to you or if your spiritual body is allowed to extend to connect with the other person.

When you are doing healing work you must be clear that the energy is coming from God. It has nothing to do with you, you are just a channel. You must have absolutely no doubt about this. You must be willing to be guided. You must keep firmly in your mind that this energy is God. Many people have trouble with this, especially people like doctors, who want to analyse it as they go along and we are not supposed to do that. We just do it because we want to do it and let it happen. How it is done is not important, it's the results that count.

If we really truly want to do something to help people, we will be guided to help them. We will be given the guidance and the ability to help when it is needed.

At Te Kuiti, New Zealand, I was doing some healing with other people in the room and there were two men standing talking to each other and discussing how some people are able to see auras. So I asked the one man if he would tell me what he could see around the patient I was working on. He could see from the other side of the room where the pain was and that it was slowly being taken away until it was gone. Then he said that there was still some pain in the left hip, so I went down there and sure enough there was some pain in the joint. So I worked on it until it went away and he was able to watch the pain go away. The next patient had problems in the abdomen and chest. The man seeing auras was able to describe what he could see and it was exactly what I could feel in my hands. When I couldn't feel any more pain, he couldn't see any more pain. This continued for several more hours and several more patients. When I asked him how long he'd been able to do this, he replied, "Only since you asked me." This shows that if we really want to help and have feelings to do so, we do get the guidance and ability we need.

Sometimes when we feel a swollen pancreas or gall bladder, it is swollen so tight that it feels like it's going to burst, the pain is the same sort of feeling as if the pain is in your own body. (The pain is located in your left hand and fingers and it feels like the pain is being drawn out by the angels.) It is so real, you can see it in your mind, the same way you can feel it. Then you feel it getting less and less until you feel nothing at all. It is the same with the thyroid gland. You feel pressure in the bloodstream in your hand. It is a bit different than the other pain, but I cannot explain it. Quite often people with swollen gall bladder and liver trouble have a lot of pain coming from that area, then when that pain is gone, your hand will be drawn up to around the pancreas. When that is clear, the hand will be drawn toward a pressure around the thyroid. Marg is a good example. She had a swollen gall bladder that caused her excruciating pain all the time and she wasn't even able to sit down. She had been to many doctors who wanted to take it out, but she did not want to do this. As I started working on her, I found pain around the gall bladder and the liver. It took a very long time to take this pain away. When I would draw it away there would be almost a poison pain or irritation. After that went away, we would work on the pancreas. Everyday we would have to keep working on taking all this pain away (because it kept returning day after day) until finally there was no more pain. There were several other things wrong with her, and they were probably the cause of the problems with the gall bladder, so if they had taken it out they would have found other problems too, which wouldn't have been fixed by surgery. Her pain was gone after a few months.

One time when I had first started healing, I was in a church in Warkworth, New Zealand, where there was a clairvoyant speaking and a man preaching on healing who had had 40 years' experience. When question time came, I asked him if he could tell me where my healing was leading me and what I was supposed to use it for, as it was developing so fast. He asked me why I felt it was developing. I replied that when I first began, I could feel cold spots in a person's aura. Now I can feel pain. He asked if I could actually feel pain from another person without touching them. When I replied yes and that I was also able to tell what kind of pain, the man answered by saying that I should not ask him or any other living person. He said that I had a gift that I should use, but no one could tell me what to do, I would just have to be guided. The thing that he did tell me was that I was going to be busy and he was proved to be right.

That same evening a healing service was held in the church and I stayed to help. The clairvoyant told me that, while I was healing, she was able to see blue lights coming from my hands and white lights coming from my fingers going right through the person I was working on. She said it would be able to stop cancer or anything. The clairvoyant also told me that she was telling me this from the spirit world and that this power was coming from somewhere a lot farther out and from somewhere they in the spirit world didn't know anything about. Therefore, I've never thought about working with guides or anything from the spirit world and since the healing energy comes to help people, I would use what comes. I just ask God for the healing energy and thank God for the privilege of being here and allowing me to transmit it. I thank Jesus for allowing us to feel and share his presence while he is guiding us and helping us.

I had never met anyone who could feel the pain in the same way as I was able to and feel exactly what it is in the person's body. However, I met a great number of people who, after working with me for a short time, were then able to feel the pain like I do and will always be able to do that. So once they get connected and are able to feel it, they will be able to do it always.

As mentioned under living at ground level and visualisation, one time when I was in Canada, I got a phone call about a girl in New Zealand who was in the hospital dying of 2 brain tumours. This was on December 17 and she was in a coma and supposed to die before Christmas. She was in terrible pain. So the family called to ask if I could help relieve the pain. Since I did not know what to do, I just prayed and asked God to guide me to feel the tumours in the girl's spiritual body. The second I prayed, I could feel her spiritual body in front of me and I could feel the two tumours in the spiritual body, one was long and the other was short, and they were sore and throbbing. I could feel the pain and the throbbing in my hand, so I took the tumours and threw them out the window behind me. I then moved my hands back to the spiritual body and I couldn't find anything but a warm glow, so I kept on praying and searching for any more problems. The energy was built up so much in the spiritual body that it started pushing my hands away. I then asked that the spiritual body be returned to its proper place. All this only took four minutes. The next day, the people phoned and told me that suddenly in the night the girl's pain had stopped and her temperature returned to normal and she was sitting up, eating a meal, and the doctors were going to let her go home for Christmas. Two weeks later, Peter rang back and said that she had been to three cancer clinics and the doctors could not find any trace of the tumours and couldn't figure out how they could make such a mistake. I have seen and heard from that girl several times since and she is still doing well and has had two children since.

It seems ridiculous to say a tumour was removed from so many miles away, but with this energy, there is no limit when it is done with prayer. With what we're using here time and distance doesn't matter. We have no idea what we can do with this energy. If one person can remove a brain tumour from 12,000 miles away, why not two people, why not ten, why not more? If we all got together, there may be no limit to what we are able to do with this energy. We have as yet no idea of how much we can do with prayers and God's help.

Every Healing Needs Guidance

There was another man who was crippled from the face down and all he could move was his eyes. For some reason he didn't recover after we worked on him. He was certainly different after the treatment and has a great outlook on life. As he lay there he could slowly move his fingers and his toes and his eyebrows. He can now use a computer with these slight movements. This man is able to spiritually uplift every person he meets. There is just something about him; it doesn't come from his body, it must come from his mind. Everybody who has ever met him will never forget him. He didn't have much feeling in his body at all when I first saw him, but by the end of the day he began to have feeling in his toes and fingers. A few days later, they were communicating with him by using his eyebrows when they pointed to certain words. He spelled out one day that he wanted to go to a rock concert. They asked him if he would like to go to this concert in 2 years time, no; in 1 years time? no; in 6 months time? no; in 1 month? no; now? yes. They lifted his bed onto a pickup truck and they took him and he had a wonderful time at the concert. It is amazing how much he can do without being able to move or even speak. That's something we will learn some day. I guess that is why he is still like this, to teach himself and others.

There are so many people who can help others and are helping others and don't even know they are doing it. A lot of nurses have the gift of healing, but never realise it and don't know how much they could do with it. You can't do anything unless you try, so if you want to help someone, for goodness sake try. If you do, you will be amazed at the results. Ask God for guidance and be guided to do what you want to do. If you feel your hands are being pulled away, let them be guided; if you feel they are giving healing power let them do it and you will be amazed at the results.

The way I am guided to heal isn't the only way although it is the way that often gets good results. After praying for guidance to help a person we cannot get advice from someone else. We have to follow the guidance we recieve. The way I feel about and think for my guidance has been influenced by my early attendance at a Christian Sunday School. I have always felt God's energy and guidance coming through the presence of Jesus Christ. Many people being healed are also able to feel his presence above us while healing is taking place. People of other religious traditions may feel the energy coming through other channels to get the same results.

It didn't seem necessary to explain how the energy was being channelled into the patient until hearing other people's stories about what they had felt and often thinking the energy was coming from me. So I want to explain that for the healing energy to flow it has to be firmly in my mind at all times that Jesus Christ is my connection to God which to me is where the healing energy comes from. In addition I have also felt that his energy would not come through me unless my respect for all nature and love for all living things was there at all times. The guidance coming to me now is to get as much as possible written down about the experiences I have been sharing so that others may benefit some day from what I have learnt. One thing is certain if we want to help someone, we cannot do anything if we don't try, and if we do try with prayer we will be amazed.

In many overseas hospitals some doctors and nursing staff are using healing prayers in their work to help the patient. This has to be done secretly in their own time as it is not approved of by the hospital administration. Prayers and kindness do not show a cash profit like drugs do even if the drugs used are of no help. We need operations and drugs, but we also need love, kindness and prayer. It is an ideal situation where they are all combined just for the good of the patient with no thought of profit. The final results are then in the hands of God.

I must mention the phantom pain which patients feel, whether it is days after the operation or years after they've had a limb removed. This pain feels different than other pains in the spiritual body because you feel it the same as in the physical body. When a person has had his arm removed, and he can feel the poison in the bloodstream, it is the same in the spiritual body. When a person has had a limb off I will gently go to the limb where all the trouble was and remove all the trouble that was there in the spiritual body. This one lady came, who had phantom pain for many years after having an arm removed and my hand drifted to the area where there was poison in the bloodstream and it took a long time to remove that pain. When it had gone, she couldn't feel the pain anymore.

A man with a wooden leg who had cancer throughout his body came to see me. My hand went immediately over the wooden leg where the cancer had started. I could feel the pain there in the spiritual body and therefore worked there in the area over the wooden leg. A woman who was working with me twice a week came in to help. She didn't know he had a wooden leg and her hands went directly to the same area over the wooden leg. We worked there until all the pain was gone. So, removing a limb is not a complete answer to any disease. Although the physical problem has gone with the removal of the limb, the disease is still there in the spiritual body and will probably start up somewhere else in the physical body.

To be able to feel with your hands, you must be completely relaxed and let your hands float over the aura, just as if you are in a bath allowing your arms to float. Your arms will float to where they are needed most and will continue to float there until the trouble is gone and they will then float somewhere else. Sometimes they may find a poison pain, a pressure pain, or a swelling. Then your hand may float somewhere else and find a different pain until all the pain is gone.

I used to always work relaxed with God until there was a warm glow around the body and that would push my hands away, as if there was a bubble around the body protecting the person. When I was working on a girl who had been molested as a child, she couldn't let anyone show her any kind of affection or get too close to her. When she finally did relax and I got a warm glow coming from her body, I was 3 feet above her and I realised that there was a white light coming down on her from directly above. She was getting all the love and comfort and healing that she needed from the right place and it wasn't upsetting her at all. That made me realise that's all I need to do. I don't need to give love and comfort myself, I just need to let the healing do it.

There are some instances which prove to me that something is being drawn out of the body. I worked on a lady who had an open ulcer on her leg that was moist and weeping and red all around. Within 7 minutes, all the redness was gone and all the moisture had gone and a layer of film, almost like skin, had covered the whole area.

Another time, there was a man with a lump of cancer on his face. I could feel my one finger being drawn to a certain place in front of his face. In a few minutes all the pus started running down his face and he had to keep wiping it off until the blood came which meant it was all clear.

One other time, there was a lady who had fluid in the lungs, so I held my hands alongside her ribs and I could feel something pulling and pulling at my hands for five minutes. There was no change that we could see, but she did feel better when I left. The next morning when I saw her, all the fluid from her lungs had come through her ribs to her skin and was lying under her skin like a big blister. Two cupfuls of fluid was there under her skin. So this proves that when you feel your hand pulling something out, something is definitely coming out of the body.

When starting we may not be able to feel pain, but may be able to feel something different like the temperature over the body. All we need to do is feel a difference in some parts then keep on working and praying until there is an even warm glow over the whole body. I never thought it was necessary to feel all the pain and it may not be, but it is nice to be able to feel exactly what the patient is feeling and know when it is going away or is all gone. I have just found out from working with a person who had muscular dystrophy that moving the fingers slowly downwards above the leg there is a feeling as if small threads of nerve pain are coming out of her leg. As the hand is drawn slowly down the leg the threads have a good grip and are removing some numbness there, but if the hand is drawn down quickly the threads will break and nothing will be removed.

Healing as reversing the process

A doctor in Canada told me he could understand what was happening with the healing. His explanation was that with the change of attitude of the patient, the immune system was now strong enough to turn the cancer cells back into normal cells, while before the cancer was the stronger and was able to turn the normal cells into cancer cells. So this was just reversing the process.

This was especially obvious when people had been taken off drugs that were weakening the immune system, but weren't doing any good towards reducing the cancer. Then with the change of attitude the patient was able to get enough of the loving healing energy that surrounds our planet to allow the immune system to take control.

At this stage I wish to make it clear that I have nothing but respect for all hospital staff, scientists and doctors and the work they are doing. I probably wouldn't be here myself now if I hadn't received Penicillin, flown daily from Australia, while in the Lavington Private Hospital about 1945. There is nothing wrong with drugs being used in the right quantity to help patients but there is a lot wrong with using them to show huge profits for the companies who make them, regardless whether they are doing the patient any good or not. Many doctors and nurses have a high concern for their patients and are willing to refer them to alternative therapies if they are not able to assist further.

There have been many millions of dollars spent over the last 40 years on research and developing drugs because there is a big profit in making them. However, not one cent of the huge amount of medical research dollars has apparently been spent on finding out why some people recover from terminal diseases on their own after a change of attitude and being able to tap into the universal energy that surrounds us. There is probably because it is all free and there is no profit except to the patient who feels the benefit.

Doctors' attitudes

My plane fare was paid by a lady in a hospital in Canada to go to spend some time with her because there was nothing medical science could do for her. Two minutes after I arrived a doctor came into the room so I sat down. He said, "No don't stop because I am interested and knew you were coming." After 20 minutes five doctors had been into the room and taken tests on the lady before and after healing.

Then one doctor said he wanted to see me before I went away. When I met him in the corridor later he said the five doctors have had a meeting and decided that although we have had many years of medical research and study you are able to do something we cannot do, and said if I would do all I could to help that lady they would do anything they could in the hospital to assist me. These doctors couldn't do this openly for fear of losing their licences. I know the day will come when nurses and doctors will openly be using this healing energy just to help the patient to heal him or herself and not to make a profit.

All over the world people are doing experiments to find out more about this healing energy that connects all living things. In Russia they had a mother rabbit in a laboratory all wired up to very sensitive machines and then took her four babies hundreds of miles away and down to the bottom of the ocean in a submarine. The mother's reaction let them know that the exact split second they killed one of the babies she knew, but there was no scientific explanation as to how that could happen.

There is so much we don't understand about this energy, like at times a person being healed from thousands of miles away. This seems impossible until you think that like the mother rabbit she was connected to the energy that created all living things and the whole universe. That ability was given to her to protect her young and it may be given to the people who want to help and protect each other and all living things. It is not given to people who intend to make big profits from the results.

Gifts: *energy and guidance will come when needed*

As mentioned before, at a healing group meeting in Te Kuiti with many people in the room, two men were talking about seeing auras. I said never mind talking about them, tell me what you can see here. One man said that the pain had almost gone about the shoulders but there was more trouble near the hip. Then as I worked on the pain in the hips he reported that it had just about gone.

As each patient took his turn on the chair for healing he would tell me where all the trouble was and when it had gone away. We worked together all day and he could see everything that I could feel that was wrong in their bodies. When finally I did get a chance to talk to him, I asked how long he had been able to see these things and he answered, "Just since you asked me." This has also happened on other occasions when people have never been able to see these things before, then suddenly they could when they wanted to help someone and dozens of times when people had never been able to feel any pain from someone else before could suddenly feel all the different kinds of pain in a person's body.

What I tell nurses and social workers is that if you want to help someone, please try, because that is the only way you will know if you can help or not, even if all the specialists say nothing can be done to help. Working with prayers there are so many miracles that do happen that cannot be explained by the specialists, they just say this was spontaneous remission, but never try to find out why it happened.

Why isn't some research done into why people go into spontaneous remission and what was the change of attitude they went through to bring this about? If research was done into what brings about the spontaneous changes a lot could be done towards preventing the diseases.

Questions I have been asked

Q. Is it necessary to pray aloud while healing?

A. From my own experience I have found it is necessary for me to keep my mind on the fact that the energy is coming from God. Prayer can assist in keeping the minds of the healer and patient on the fact that the energy is coming from God.

The reason I say this, is that while working in a room where there are other people talking often the energy going through my hands becomes weaker, probably because unconsciously I am hearing what others are saying. Then when I ask God to let his healing power go through my hands to help this person the patient will give a jump and ask what happened, and to me it is just like turning on an electric light switch. This allows me to feel the energy flow through my hands and through the patient again.

Because I have to keep my mind on the fact that the healing energy is coming directly from God I do think it must help if the patient also realises where the loving energy is coming from. After praying aloud for this reason over a period it was found that a big percentage of the patients would ask for the prayers because they felt they were an important part of the healing.

Through praying to myself all the time while healing I am able to feel the love and healing energy going through my hands into the patient and at the same time feel the pain and the cause of the pain coming away from the body. Therefore it seems necessary for the patient and the healer to realise that the heart love and the healing energy they feel is coming from God and they are sharing God's love with each other and the angels that are present.

The gift of healing is to glorify God so if we are willing to accept his healing it seems right that we give thanks to him while we are making use of his gift.

Q. What is the role of the Healer, and why can't the Angels do it on their own?

A. The only reason seems to be that God wants us to have love and respect for each other. If we have love and respect for all things, we will also come to have love and respect for all living things and all he created.

The message I want people to get is this. If you do have sympathy, love and respect for someone suffering and you would like to make things easier for them, please try. We can't do anything unless we try. By asking for guidance first you will be amazed at the results you get, but more amazing is the benefit you receive yourself. No matter how hard we try to help others we always get more back in return, in so many different ways, even though all our intentions were just to help the other person.

Q. Does energy come through the left or right hand?

A. My own experience is that it is only possible for me to feel pain or anything else from the patient's body if I feel it with the left hand without touching the body and the loving healing energy only goes in through my right hand.

This seems to be the same for most people, but whether it is the same for everyone I am not sure. It is rather odd but the right and left hand functions appear reversed with active cancer. By putting my right hand on a person with cancer I can feel a hot burning feeling while the cancer is active, but after a few days of healing there is no more heat.

Then we know it is not active any more. Holding the right hand on it, it is possible to feel a tumour growing softer and smaller. But with my left hand on the same place I don't feel any heat whether it is active or not.

Visualisation does work

(Warkworth, New Zealand)

In New Zealand we had a young calf that was so sick it was hard to see if it was breathing or not. Its mouth was cold inside and it couldn't move at all. We had done everything advised by the vet but nothing worked. It wouldn't suck at all, but if I held its head up and put a little bit of warm milk in its mouth it would swallow. This made me decide that as long as it would do that I would feed it every two hours day and night.

This was done for many days, but it did not show any sign of improvement. Then one day a lady phoned me to say she had just heard that while doing healing it was a good idea to always visualise your patient as being fit and well while working on them.

After I heard that I decided to think of the calf as being well from then on. This calf was in a hay barn away from the house and my daughter used to often come with me to do anything she could, such as turning it over often and keeping its bed dry and comfortable.

At one o'clock in the morning it gave two sucks on my finger so gently they were hardly felt, next feed it gave two more gentle sucks and moved its tongue slightly. This was a definite improvement. By daybreak it was really trying to suck and would drink all I was willing to give it. Then all day it was hungry and trying to move, and by nightfall it was on its feet again.

Next morning we put it back on the cow and it seemed to be doing well, but after a few days all its hair started falling out, and by the end of the week it was all sunburnt and the skin was cracking in many places. These cracks were moist and weeping. We got the vet's advice again and were told we would have to kill it because nothing would make the hair grow at this stage. It would get pneumonia and would die.

Wendy and I decided we were not going to give up that easily after all it had been through. That night we both concentrated on thinking of it covered in hair again. Next morning it seemed a bit different, but I thought it must be my imagination. However, the next day there was a very fine fluff all over it and a few days later it was covered in hair again.

It was hard to believe and there was nothing else that could have made any difference but our visualisation. I don't mind if people don't believe what I say because I find it hard to believe myself even though I do see hundreds of miracles and know nothing is impossible.

Suggestions for healing

In the many years I have been involved in healing since the little bird incident the healing has often been completely successful and many times partly successful. At other times the pain or trouble may keep coming back every day. These variations can be for many reasons.

The patients who have a complete cure are the ones who have a complete change of attitude. They leave everything completely to God, concentrate on being guided by their hearts and appreciating every moment of every day while they are here. This has all been done by leaving my mind completely blank and concentrating on the energy coming through my hands, knowing it is coming from above just for the special purpose of helping the patient.

While your mind is firmly on that alone, one hand (with me it is the left) will act as an in-built body scanner. In fact it will scan the physical body and the Aura (or energy around the physical body). For me, it will not only detect where any trouble is, but I can actually feel any pain and know if it is in the bone, joint, muscle, nerve, intestines or blood stream, and if it is an infection, or swelling in any particular organ, tube, or area.

This has always been my method of working but it can be upset by many reasons, mainly because the patient does not have a complete change of attitude and be guided by their heart. Many things can impede this process. The patient may still keep on trying other things, or working with other people who use a different method or energy. The patient may keep on working with someone else, who is using crystals or other methods or have a crystal on their body or near them. The energy that comes through me and crystals do not work well together.

Others may have a change of attitude at the time, but may have another change after talking with someone who does not understand the energy that is shared between the healer and the patient or the change in attitude that can result.

There have been many people who could feel all the same things as I could, but lost it again after trying different methods and trying to analyse what they were doing—using their head instead of their heart. They were not concentrating on the energy coming from God through their hands just for the special purpose of helping the patient.

The healing energy seems to mainly come through the hands. So when some people are experimenting, by putting their hands palm to palm even when not touching, they are just turning different energy back on themselves. Focus the mind on where the energy is coming from (God) and let the energy flow through just for the benefit of the patient. So many people have the ability to be able to feel everything in a person's body, but lose it again, probably through not always keeping in mind that it is coming through them just for the purpose of helping the patient.

While Dr. Wilson of the Foundation for the Study of Subtle Energies was doing his research he found some were losing their ability when their ego or the dollar sign came into their minds.

Unfortunately, even when the healer does everything right, the patient must have a change of attitude for the healing to be effective. This allows the immune system to build up, and become strong enough to be able to turn diseased cells back into normal cells, and the patient then shows signs of improvement.

Other peoples' influences can allow the patient to turn back and recreate their diseases. No amount of healing will be permanent if this is happening.

It seems to be a very gentle balance in the person's mind, that allows them to overcome their disease or recreate it. Prayers can turn that balance the right way.

EPILOGUE

Letter to Eve and others in need

Dear Eve

This is just a note to say you have been in my prayers and I have been sending you healing prayers also.

Enclosed are a few papers to let you know what I have been doing with the gift God has given me.

Over the last five years I have been working with many doctors all over America and Canada, mostly on terminally ill patients. I have seen so many miracles that it is plain that nothing is impossible. Although there are some people who are so special that God wants them for some special purpose. Casey was one of these and was taken with leukemia at five years of age. Still, in eight days he taught me more than any one had ever been able to. Enclosed is a letter from his Father.

This is being typed out although I still don't know how to find your address. It is also a message just for you and not for any publicity.

I would be willing to come and meet you some day, but in the meantime do know that with healing prayers the distance doesn't matter. I have been sending healing prayers for almost six weeks now.

May God bless you and may the power of his love, that is coming directly into you from the prayers of people from all over the world, be so strong that you will be so full of his love it will shine out of you and help anyone who comes in contact with you.

Most of the miracles that I have seen are with people who have decided to leave everything to God and be grateful and enjoy every moment while they are here—every breath of fresh air, every moment of sunshine, every flower and every bird, insect or blade of grass—and they are still enjoying them all six years later.

You have touched the hearts of thousands of people and every hour of every day you will touch and help more and more. You have already done more than most people could possibly do even if they lived to be over 100 years old.

The one message that I am trying to send to people is that love, kindness, respect for all living things and prayers are worth more than anything in the world.

Once again, May God bless you.

Rod Campbell

APPENDIX I - Stories involving Rod Campbell

Dona Williamson's story

(Springfield, Missouri)

ROD CAMPBELL—From a Church newsletter by Dona Williamson

"It is not I, but the Father who dwells within me who does his works."

There's a modern-day stranger among us who's repeating some familiar phrases. Born December 17, 1914, in Gisborne, New Zealand, Rod Campbell, recalls a time in 1957 when a horse fell on him breaking his back. Suffering other multiple breaks, three bone grafts, and broken ribs due to a falling tree, Rod is no stranger to pain and suffering. Where medicine failed, he felt he was healed through the prayers of others.

An experience with his daughter and a young bird that had been captured by a cat reinforced his belief that God can heal through prayer and genuine love, concern and kindness from another. Now, at 75, he's wanting to bring healing to those he can, teach others to be able to do the same, and network his healing news to those who share like views—pooling their knowledge, gifts, and information.

Moving to Calgary, Canada, four years ago, he began devoting his full time to healing those who had lost hope in modern medicine and "approved" practices. A spring visit to the Springfield area was so impressive that he has now relocated to our more central locale. (Springfield, Missouri).

Friends and church people have spread the word and are keeping him busy sharing his philosophy and demonstrating his techniques between his writing. He works on a donation basis, trusting God to take care of his needs.

Rod explains that his left hand seems to act as a receiver or magnet for pain and disease, while he uses his right hand to direct the healing energy which he feels coming from above. He uses the two alternately to achieve a state of balance in the body.

As he runs his left hand through one's "auric" space, he feels in his hand whatever is happening in the body. If the problem is in the blood, then he feels a sensation in his blood. If there is pain in the bones, then he feels it in the bones of his hand, etc. As he tunes into the problem, his left hand works at drawing the troubled energy out. He gathers the pain which seems to stick to his hand and periodically flips it away.

He reports experiences with healing "in absentia" where he has prayed for the auric body of the person desiring the healing to be present. He then proceeds to work on that body using the above process and then prays for its healing and safe return to the healee.

Rod feels that many recover from "fatal" diseases, because of the way treatment is given "with love, kindness, and respect" and because an attitude change takes place in the person. "When a cancer patient is told he has two weeks to live, things he has been worrying about in the past are not important any more," Rod explains. The spiritual becomes more important than the material realm. "The cause of the cancer is gone, and they become more determined to overcome the cancer and the body then starts turning the cancer cells back into normal cells." A change in outlook results in basic attitude changes.

I have attended several of the group demonstrations Rod has given and he is one of the most sincere and kindest people genuinely concerned with the welfare of others that I have ever met.

Rod, we behold the Christ within you giving us a unique example of how love, kindness, and concern for our fellowman can enhance life for us all.

Love and respect—Moose Potter

(Springfield, Missouri)

"LOVE AND RESPECT FOR ALL LIVING THINGS"—ROD CAMPBELL'S FIRST LAW— From a Church newsletter by Moose Potter

When I first met Rod Campbell I was living the aftermath of a sudden shotgun sequence of events ending with a recent right mastectomy. In short, I was trapped in a nightmare: angry, confused, in pain, in shock, exhausted—terrified. The days, minutes, and seconds of my existence since diagnosis had been tinged with an undercurrent of black fear and dread. Endless senseless questions had tormented me, all without answers. Why me who so zestfully loves life? Why now this death sentence for one too young with so much living still ahead? Why cancer? It could never happen to me! Why? Why? Why?

And then—curious and rather sceptic, I admit—one evening I found myself in the presence of this remarkable man, idly watching the beauty of his hands in motion over me as I lay on his healing table. Soon I became aware that what he was doing felt wonderful—that it was life-important for me to be there at that moment drawing gentleness, unaffected simplicity, healing. I tuned into a warm, wonderful tingling in my solar plexus that grew into a sense of well-being for the first time in weeks. Later that night I went home and slept deeply and untroubled with dread.

And slowly over the next months I grew to know that I was going to be all right.

Rod heals by simply being what he is: love and respect for all living things. He is his message. In fact, the first time I saw him I kept wanting to say— kept feeling the words, "kinship with All Life." I have since come to know that this phrase embodies the core of what he wants all of us to know. All healing done with love, kindness and power—to change a person's life, to make a terminally ill patient recover, or to let him die completely at peace with no pain.

Rod relates a potent and moving illustration of this point expressed in a recent article written by a doctor of his experience in a hospital—as a patient. Dripping with sweat, he had lain in his bed for endless hours, enduring terrible pain that defied an arsenal of medication. He marvelled that he had treated patients for years, yet had absolutely no conception of what pain was like. And then a cleaning lady working in his room ignored the rules and performed a miracle that could have cost her her job; instead it healed a life and changed forever a doctor's method of treating his patients. This lady simply and very lovingly ran a cool, damp cloth over his agonised body. Immediately he felt better, then astounded when he realised the awful pain was completely and suddenly gone! That simple expression of love and caring had gone way beyond the cold, impersonal—and expensive—technology and medicine and doctors to tap the universal source of all healing. It was an experience he would never forget. Never again would he treat a patient with anything other than compassion and love as he practiced medicine.

Rod feels this kinship with life happening with all living things. Dogs have been known to bring kittens home so they will be cared for when the mother cat is unable to do so; birds pull injured companions off roads to safety; rabbits pull dead cohorts out of traffic ways and then sit by them for days; horses and dogs will lead humans to aid another animal caught in a fence or a swamp. He sees the potential for love and respect among and between all levels of existence as limitless.

From early childhood Rod has felt a connection—a oneness—with all life. When healing he visualises himself as forming a direct channel of God's power, thereby tapping this universal source of unity and love. It is Rod's belief that Guidance has led him here to Springfield in order to sow seeds of Love, Contentedness, and Compassion that will grow into healed lives. Ultimately he feels it will be these transformed people themselves that will do most of the work of spreading the message for him.

And, indeed, I see myself as one of these ripples. Already most of the seemingly senseless questions that originally had plagued me now have answers—positive, comforting, solid ones. Slowly I am changing my lifestyle, my very being. Using Rod's example I am becoming what I want my life to be. In short, I am healing my soul, my body, my life; therefore, there is every likelihood that my physical cure will be permanent. But, most importantly, I am working toward the point where I can honestly and joyfully say that cancer is one of the best things that has ever happened to me —whatever the physical outcome.

Zestfully I join the hundreds of others whose lives have been touched— therefore transformed and healed by Rod Campbell. Let the great adventure begin—for all of us!

Sanctuary house—Mr Howell

(Snowmass, Colorado)

My wife, Barbara, and I moved to Colorado just before Christmas, 1986. We wanted to live in the Old Snowmass valley, near Saint Benedict's Monastery. But we had little funds with which to even begin to buy a house. Yet we looked anyway, if for no other reason than to take drives and see the countryside.

I had my first decent job in years and we thought we might be able to afford something in the $80,000 range, if we found an understanding lending institution. But the homes in "our valley" were at least 50% higher than that figure. Real estate agents were showing us homes further to the north and we considered a few but they didn't hold us, especially since Barbara's inner guidance had revealed to her that we would find a house and that, "it would be as if coming up out of the ground." We thought that must mean a tepee, a tree fort, or at best a log cabin.

I remember in March, we drove up to Gateway Mesa, overlooking "our valley," and thought it offered a grand view. But the snow was heavy on the ground and, winding down the then dirt road, Barbara said, "You couldn't pay me enough to live here." That April, after the spring melt, a friend who did real estate on the side showed us a house half way up Gateway Mesa. If it wasn't for us getting back in the car I wouldn't have noticed in her listings book, that there were three homes for sale on the top of the mesa. One was too expensive, one lacked charm, but the moment I walked down the drive of a two-part house burned into the ground, I knew it was ours.

I'll never forget seeing the view and thinking that this somewhat unfinished house with its lovely roof line, offered for $119,500 must be $1,119,500, and that the listings book had made a mistake. Right away I pointed down to the lower patio out of which a darling juniper rose out of a bed of Cerastium by a huge heart-shaped hot tub and said, "That's where we're going to be married."

In July, having had an offer of $100,500 accepted, we moved in, renting the house until we could close. I had already started sculpting the terrain for a lawn I was laying and making a stone staircase for Barbara's bridal entrance, feeling that this indeed was our home. Barbara's inner voice has proven true, and ever since we had moved to Colorado she had wanted, "a house with a retreat house in the Old Snowmass valley." And that's exactly what we had. Yet we wondered how in heaven's name we would afford it, let alone convince a bank to give us a loan.

Our first guest offered to co-sign our first mortgage. Our third guest bought our second mortgage through his business, so we wouldn't have to go through the loan, as had its underwriters. On the day the bank was supposed to give its final verdict, our real estate agent called to say that our buying the house looked "very black" and that she was heartbroken.

That afternoon I heard the phone ring close to 5 PM. "How are you, Mr. Howell?" a female voice from the bank said, "Okay," I replied, fearing the words that would send us packing. "I'm just calling to tell you, Mr. Howell, that your loan has been approved." I threw my tools in the air and shouted the news to Barbara. To this day we have no idea what made the bank change its mind. We closed in August and were married in September, a joyous time, despite the fact that a week before I had lost my job and two weeks later we had a chimney fire, but it gave us new carpet we couldn't have afforded.

My mother helped us until I got work again; a part-time teaching position which allowed us to scrape by. I worked on landscaping the 1.1 acre property, already gorgeous with 800 year old junipers and a view of 40 miles of Rocky Mountains.

In the spring of 1989, we drove to Saint Louis to see my mother. She wanted to help us with our house, which we were in fear of losing, barely keeping up our payments as we were. She took us to meet her lawyer, a tall and imposing man, who grilled us about how we were going to make ends meet and pay off whatever loan she might make to us. Suddenly I found myself saying, "Look, we don't know what will happen; all we know is that this house is a miracle; God gave this property to us and we are stewards for as long as God wishes us there." The lawyer said, "'Miracle', I like that word," and the next thing I knew he was working out a way for my mother to give us the $100,000 to pay off our house completely. I never thought she had any money, so frugal she is and how simply she lives.

We continued our trip to Chicago, seeing a friend. We also saw a movie called *Field of Dreams*, the main line of which is, "If you build it, he will come." We then drove toward Omaha to visit more dear friends, and just as we crossed over into Iowa, where the movie was filmed, my chest grew heavy and I could hardly breathe. Barbara had asked me what I felt our next step with our house and our spiritual journeys was. I found myself weeping, weeping out of joy because the strongest inner message, like my own voice yet not my own, had said that our property was sacred and was to be a place of healing. Six more times I gasped and then wept, Barbara now having to drive, as it was revealed that we were to teach Christian mysticism as well as respecting all paths to God, have a library, minister especially to people who want to serve but are in a "dark night of the soul," and that our retreat house, where we already were taking overflow retreatants from the monastery, would, by the very spiritual power inherent in the property, and the vision that we were receiving, nurture and redirect such persons into paths that would greatly benefit them and others. I was "told" about two books I should write and we also received as part of this vision a message that we should start a small spiritual community, and that this place would be called *Sanctuary House*.

That fall we were given a scholarship to Harmonia Mundi, a conference of spiritual luminaries from the five major traditions. Wanting to go, yet still concerned about spending the very last of our savings, we remembered the Parable of the Talents and decided to invest in our spiritual yearnings. There we received a blessing from the Dalai Lama, met a Sufi Sheik who has become a vital friend, and received our first donation to begin building a chapel and meditation / prayer hall which would connect our retreat house with our house. And the day after we returned the monastery lent us its back hoe and a dear friend was digging the foundation, donating half his time.

Though the structure was largely finished by December, it would take a year and a half before we would begin on the interior. A man came to us, whom we felt called to invite to live with us, and be in our community. He stayed on causing many difficult months and we accomplished little else other than finding how challenging it was to live in the community. However, as well as teaching a number of small courses on Centering Prayer and continuing our retreat house work, we did enjoy that year the presence of two Buddhist lamas, our Sufi sheik, Frs. Theophane and Thomas Keating from Saint Benedict's Monastery, as well as several gifted healers, and we packed up to 40 people in our small living room.

But, taking a pilgrimage to Chimayo, New Mexico, for Christmas 1990, Barbara and I rekindled the primacy of the vision that had been given us. How the meditation hall would be finished was a complete mystery, yet by spring Barbara had decided that on her 50th birthday in August we would dedicate our meditation hall. Shortly after that, the next major donation was received from a woman we had met only hours before. So we prayed that the right carpenters would come, and indeed we were guided to someone who had built a meditation hall some years previously.

The finishing of the hall was revelatory, since we had only the vague parameters of its design in mind. And what happened can best be described only as the day-by-day revelation of what the meditation hall itself wanted to be. Two more donations, again offers out of the blue, were received, coupled by gifts of sculpture and weaving and donations of time and various expertise until the result was, in all humility, a work of art divinely wrought. We dedicated it, in the presence of nearly 80 friends, some of whom had come from as far as Seattle, to the healing work of The Lord who had made us stewards of this vision, on August 18, 1991, a day of fullness and simple glory. Indeed, a deer (I had not seen one before where we live) sat on an adjacent hillside and watched, offering a gentle but very potent blessing, for over three hours, leaving only after meditation and Mass.

That was a Sunday. Monday we cleaned up, and on Tuesday Rod Campbell came to do healings, wishing to come at least once a month. The meditation hall couldn't wait to begin to be used for the healing work God had intended.

We will offer Centering Prayer sittings twice daily, one Saturday a month and one weekend a season, as well as continuing to make *Sanctuary House* available to retreatants and to spiritual teachers and healers, as well as to those in need of healing and prayer.

Rod's comments on this story:

"I didn't know anything about this centre being built and didn't know why I had to ring Barbara that morning while in that area. Five people from all over the U.S.A. had come for the opening and were all packed ready to go home, but when they were told I was coming down they decided to stay another day.

"We had two full days healing there and it was amazing to see the change in some of the patients, especially the two brain damaged children and the young wolf that was also brought for healing.

"This is a beautiful place and I would like to see others like it all over the world. In the meantime it would be a good idea to give all the support to these people who are trusting in God and working so hard just to help others.

"Am looking forward to seeing many more like this in many areas."

Rod Campbell.

Personal experience of Frank Kemeri

(Calgary, Alberta)

In December 1989 during a routine medical examination, twenty eight year old Frank Kemeri discovered he had Hodgkin's disease. Further tests revealed stage III B.

In February Frank began chemotherapy, at the same time he began seeing Rod Campbell. Without knowing where the tumours were or at what stage, he ran his hands over Frank's body and was able to tell him exactly where they were. X-rays confirmed this.

After the first session alone, the tumours had shrunk to smaller than half the original size. By the second session they were barely visible.

Frank continued to see Rod Campbell every couple of months for about two years after that . On a separate instance he had a white blood count of 11 the day before he went to Mr. Campbell. The next day he had blood work done again and white blood count was back to 6 (normal).

Five years later Frank is married with a child and looks to be in perfect health and is really appreciating all the good things in life.

Extracts—"The Transits of Consciousness"—Edgar Wilson

(Boulder, Colorado)

In fact, after all my years of looking at brain waves, I have yet to find that consciousness even exists in the head. We may just be sending messages, commands, to set up the resonances to get the muscles moving, the digestive juices going, but we really don't live in our brain.

We seem to create a fundamental illusion of time and space of concentrating very narrow-focused alpha activity in the back of the head. The fairly stable spatio-temporal nature of the alpha in many rigid personalities creates the illusion of certainty because it temporarily overwhelms the seeming chaos of multiple stimuli. This allows us to concentrate on learned signals and values. I started to find out about five years ago that sound made a noticeable difference in brain-wave patterns. I could get people to change brain patterns with sounds. We began to see people change states of consciousness, particularly when I used binaural beat frequencies, which I'd heard of from the work of Robert Monroe who had measured changes in the brain with these frequencies since 1957, but there were no references. Then I started giving the individual feedback with the sound of his own brain waves. Now we could get him to track more complex information relative to the interactions of different frequencies in different places. He began to do things with his brain waves that he should not have been able to according to the scientific literature. For example, his temporal lobes would light up in theta when listening to soul-moving music.

Another thing I found at this time was that I, as the researcher; had a profound effect on the actual outcome of the experiment I was running. So I began to work on myself. I began working with holotropic breathwork and hyperventilating to intense music and found that I had feelings, something I'd forgotten for thirty years. When you practice medicine you grow calluses around your soul, so that you can tolerate the pain of other people. Opening that up was no small issue. When I began to feel again, my own brain waves changed. Now I could light up my temporal lobes. I had greased a transit I'd forgotten I had. The research process began to unfold. To change their states of consciousness, people had to be free to follow their feelings. They had to feel this was legitimate; otherwise, all I recorded was novelty response—more alpha. Now, as I stimulated them with sound that encouraged emotion and feeling, I began to find changes that would occur in the brain as a direct response to the stimulus I was feeling into the brain.

That process led to an understanding about the first indication of transcendent experience. Time/space awareness is the first thing to disappear when one is moving into a transcendent or dissociate state. Dissociative states occur when you lose awareness of time/space. Heightened activity seems to happen right in the middle of the head—the crown chakra if you like—an increase in power occurs at the point of opening oneself to what is, instead of what ought to be in the future or what should have been in the past. It's the moment of "Aha—I exist in this moment—now, and now keeps changing. I can't go back, I can't go forward, I can only exist in this moment." And suddenly a shift starts to happen as time/space is transcended. The correlation between the crown chakra and heightened activity in Cz occurs during healing with the healer, and in other transcendent states in nonhealers as well as healers.

Next I started studying healers, and found that they tended to drive people into this time/space warp when they were working with them, if there was great congruence between the healer and the healee. One day Rod Campbell, a seventy-seven-year-old from New Zealand, came to Boulder. He's an old cowpoke who discovered twenty-five years ago he had something about his hands that could transmit healing energy to others. He could reduce you to tears; he was so sincere; he had nothing to prove and he wasn't trying to make money. He was too simple, and simple people bothered me because I couldn't explain what they were doing. Rod would hold his hands over someone, who would feel warmth, vibration, energy moving, particularly if we put Rod in a more natural environment, such as a cabin in the mountains. There, where it was warm inside and the belief systems were congruent, the tears would start and suddenly something would change.

We had brain-wave measuring sensors on both Rod and the healee, and we would switch back and forth between the two. I also had a magnetometer above Rod's head. He made beautiful spikes of ascending frequency and power as he went into his healing mode. I'd say, "Rod you can heal him now," and he would do it; I'd say, "Rod you can stop," and he would. He said it just came through him. When Rod was working on someone, the subject's distribution and amplitude of dominant alpha would change towards the healer's brain wave pattern, and change back to baseline when he'd finished. Rod was experiencing high frequency and power in his brain activity, and everything else was shut down. Something was happening here, in very high frequencies, with no evidence of change in alpha, beta or theta. My rational mind was really boggled by all this—I kept trying to explain it away.

It seems that suddenly there's a shift from the centre of the head out to the temporal areas as you go from the loss of time/space awareness to an awareness of deep empathy, those moments in our lives—only moments for most of us—when we lose the sense of separateness from each other and from our world. Those are the moments when we are able to strip away that last little vestige of fear, to know that we are part and parcel of the same stuff, transcendent stuff. We saw also that this was accompanied by low-frequency occurrences, 1 to 6 Hz, in the centre of the head. This seems to keep time/space at bay; it's almost as if we go to sleep to our past and our expectations. *You get a higher frequency as you move into a transcendent state.* There's a splitting, similar to a state that you might see in a paranoid personality who can't fit into our world, where he's not accepted for his splitting. How ironic it is that we, who are frozen into our alpha state, trying to be appropriate, to learn everything there is to learn, are willing to come to a place of learning to pay money to learn how to split! In the healer experiments, this splitting occurred at a very profound level. At the time, I checked all Rod's physical functions (eye movement, respiration, heart rate), and none of them was active in affecting the brain waves. Rod was making deep, slow waves, drawing you down into a comfortable state—and then splitting you off where you could play. It was both weird and wonderful.

These phenomena, which would happen only in brief bursts, would occur with a really slow frequency to begin with and track the frequencies of the Monroe tapes in a proportional fashion as far as we could measure. The normal brain wave frequencies, delta, theta, alpha, beta, are hardly ever more than 20 microvolts power. Rod's frequencies—18 to 32 microvolts; 32 to 64 Hz at 29.9 microvolts; 64 to 128 HZ at 39 microvolts, were totally out of the range we'd ever looked at before. The temporal lobes alone were lit up—there's nothing holding the person down, no theta-delta—it's all in the temporal lobes in high frequency.

Interestingly, people who channel, who have psychic activity, but cannot remember the content of their channelling or their psychic experience, seem to light up the right temporal lobe only. Those that bring back the content of their experience seem to light up both left and right together.

APPENDIX II - Letters to Rod Campbell

Bird story—Curtis A Smith

Chicago Public Schools,
Office of Instructional Services,
1819 West Pershing Road,
Chicago, Illinois 60609
+1-312-890-8250

Ted D. Kimbrough, General Superintendent of Schools
Adrienne Y. Bailey, Deputy Superintendent

October 7, 1991

Rod Campbell, Man of Love

It was a cool and clear Saturday evening, that Rod Campbell and Cassie Zellner demonstrated their amazing abilities to transmit God's healing energy to one of God's children. The person to receive this energy was a minister from Chicago, Illinois. While Rod and Cassie were working with the minister, I stood in the other room and looked out of the window of the Holiday Inn in Harvey, Illinois. Soon a group of birds flew over the top of the Inn and perched in the tree across from Rod Campbell's room. Every minute or so, another group of birds came from various directions and landed in one of two trees outside of Rod's window. Within ten minutes, there were at least 400 birds in these two trees chirping, singing, and seemingly rejoicing at the healing that was taking place in room 414.

Could it be my imagination? Why would so many birds come from so many directions and perch in these two trees? There were many trees in the area, why these two trees? Do birds know something that man does not know? Who is more in tune with nature, man or the birds? These were some of the questions that came across my mind. Of course, I knew the answers. We are all one with God, one with life. But some have forgotten who and what they are. We are all part of the source of all life, God.

The birds knew something spectacular was going to happen and wanted to be part of this event. They seemed to have a collective consciousness that drew them to this spot, at this time.

I remember the story about the little bird that Rod held in his hand with nothing but love in his heart for the bird. A cat had caught the bird and was trying to eat him; however, Rod's daughter rescued the little bird who was near death. After a few minutes in Rod's hand, the little bird was well and flew away. As soon as the bird left Rod's hand, over thirty other birds came flying down to meet it, making a terrific noise. Then for an hour they sat up in the trees singing and rejoicing and flying down to this magnificent man from New Zealand. No prayer of thanks could have ever been said more gratefully.

Every now and then a man is born with so much love in his heart that just to be in his presence is to feel that love and feel the healing energies of the universe. Yes, the minister from Chicago received the healing that he needed. To God be the Glory.

Rod works with an associate named Cassie Zellner. Together they make a unique and powerful team to do God's work. They both are quick to tell anyone that they cannot heal. Only God can heal. They are just instruments or channels for God.

Rod states that he has seen hundreds of miracles and knows that with love, kindness, prayer, and God's help, nothing is impossible. When your health is not perfect, love and kindness are worth all of the money in the world.

Signed, Curtis A. Smith Ed.D
Retired Administrator

Our Children . . . Our Future

Major change in attitude needed for healing

The Shealy Institute
1328 East Evergreen Street
Springfield, MO 65803-4400
(417) 865-5940
Fax (417) 865-6111

March 7, 1994

Rod Campbell
PO Box 212
Warkworth
NEW ZEALAND

Dear Rod:

Thank you very much for your letter of January 4 and the booklet.

Yes indeed, you are most welcome to include the name of the clinic and my name in the book.

Obviously any patient who is willing to read the book might get the message. One never knows what will trigger the major change in attitude that is often needed to make people come around. I certainly agree with you that Love, Kindness, and Prayer can create miracles. Unfortunately I wish they were more common than they seem to be. Olga Worrall used to say that nobody ever got cured with a single shot of insulin, and most people don't get cured with a single shot of spiritual healing, primarily because they recreate their illness with their unfinished business.

I will pass the book along to Kathy Farmer since she and Pam would be the two most likely to intervene in getting patients to read your book and change their attitude.

Yes, I was sorry to hear about Dr. Wilson, which I had heard from other sources.

Our love and best wishes.
Sincerely,

C. Norman Shealy, M.C., Ph.D.

CNS/jrd
d/3/4/94
t/3/7/94

Cancer can be cured—Bob Valkenburg

Dr. J. (Bob) Valkenburg

M.D., L.A.M., M.R.I.N.

30 Hill Street, Te Kuiti

P.O. Box 39, Tel (07) 8 788-499

9th of June 1994

CANCER CAN BE CURED!

There appears to be a change emerging, throwing its first hesitant light over the horizon. Are we reaching the state of the 'hundredth Monkey?' A tendency to start asking questions. There are so many questions to ask!

Considering, we live on a tiny Planet, miles away from our small Sun, somewhere in the outskirts of a reasonably size Galaxy, called 'the Milky Way', when I discussed this many, very many!, years ago with my Father, who was a Physicist, we were all aware, that there were at least two more to be found in our Universe, 'the two clouds of Magellan', not a problem here, as they are visible with the naked eye.

Now we know that there are billions of Galaxies in a Timeless, infinite Universe, where Past and future are without limits. We can thus 'Go back to the Future', or 'go forward to the Past'.

Where does this leave us? Sitting on our little Speck, not more than Cosmic Dust, fighting, gathering more Land, gold, etc., only for more Power, ignoring the fact, that we, all of us, are just Caretakers of this minute Corner in our infinite Kosmos! Let us concentrate on this Timeless Entity where we live in, where we are a Part of, who gives endless electromagnetic Energy, in the form of never-ending 'interchange of Atoms', which includes US! Consequently, as immense Energy field between the Electron[s], in orbit around the [multi] loaded Proton, named an "ATOM", floats through every living Soul, organic matter, beyond everything, into infinity!

It encompasses our total Body, our Organs, our auto-immune system and communicates, interchanges and controls, within a healthy vibrating Environment. It maintains the Electro-Chemical Balance, under the umbrella of this ever watching AUTO-IMMUNE-SYSTEM!

Looking at our deforestation, our pesticides and herbicide poisoning going on, not to forget the disasters after our 'cleverness' had taught us, how to split the Atom and thus use the immense Energy to kill and destroy, including long time effect on our Protective System. Our pure ignorance and greed is the main cause of changes in our chemical, hence, also Physical cell structure.

This all leads to Rod Campbell, a remarkable man. He not only discovered the Radiating Energy, flowing through his hands, he also learned from within, how to use the Energy to heal and help others.

He started Healing. Rod had already a long time been communicating with his Farm animals and detected their vast Electromagnetic Energy. 'God has given me the Knowledge to use this Power for the benefit of others!' He remained at all times humble and gentle.

This inner, cosmic Voice, from our Spiritual, timeless Eternity, had told him, to use this Energy to help. This is the way, Rod works!

Rod and I have been friends for quite some time. I have watched him working. Rod is a 'born', genuine Healer, with Love and Compassion! He can heal, as we also know the results from Patients and eyewitness reports. We have the Scientific knowledge, that Electromagnetic currents, play uninterrupted roles in the fine-lanced performance, this Body of ours needs. Do micro-organisms, viral invasions, poisons, alien radiation (powerlines, TV, etc.,), atomic power plant leakage also, disturb this intricate balance, by causing bacterial or viral mutations, destroying our Auto immune system, then we become ill. Even distress, unhappiness will cause weakening of the Protective Policing in our body. Dr. Royal Raymond Rife (Roy)—(Rife's 'Polarised light Microscope' and 'Frequency Instruments'). Selective destruction of bacteria, by exposing them to specific Electromagnetic frequencies. (1953) These Quantums of Electro-Magnetic Radiation, were here created 'by Rife's brilliant invention, the frequency-Instrument. All of us however, do possess forms of extremely low-energy electromagnetic waves. Only a few of us are aware of this, even less will be able to use this invaluable cosmic Power for ultimate **HEALING!**

LOVE KINDNESS AND PRAYER, combined with the COSMIC ELECTROMAGNETIC ENERGY, radiating from your HANDS CAN PERFORM MIRACLES.

My paper started derailing. Was obvious time to turn the letter over. I hope and trust that I have been able to relay to you Rod, what I wanted to say.

I hope and expect you will still be in Warkworth, so you will receive this in time. Let us know what your plans are, that we know where you are and where next to find you.

On the back of this letter you will find a copper engraving from Greetje Pieck, an old niece of mine. She died age 19 in the year 1918, from the 'Spanish Flu'. She and her sister Adrie Pieck, an oil painter who lived to 1982, were always in forests, surrounded at all time by forest animals, deer, rabbits, cats, toads, etc. I often played around there and painted, with Adrie helping and teaching me.

I will finish this letter now and get ready for the post. Keep well Rod, and if you need anything, I can help you with, then please let me know.

Give also my best wishes to Maureen. Hope to see you both again in the near future. Wish you further success with the follow up of your first book, will look forward to read that as well!

With kindest Greetings, Yours Sincerely,

Signed Bob

The healed become healers—Shawn Verrier

26 September 1990

Whitehorse
Yukon YIA359

Hello Rod

I'm the woman from Whitehorse who brought you the Kiwi fruit that Sunday at Verda Hoilands.

It really isn't important that you put a face to a name in this case. I'm not even sure why I'm being prompted to write except to express my gratitude to you for furthering my own healing process which in turn enables me to share that healing energy with others.

I'm always full of respect for those like yourself, who put themselves out there on the edge, living so much in the moment. You certainly radiate much love and caring and I hope I was able to reflect some of that back to you.

There is within Whitehorse and the Yukon in general a good number of people of similar persuasion when it comes to healing. Your presence provided us the space to come together, to generate a lot of energy, to grow and to love one another. Thank you my friend ... I was touched.

God Bless You and Keep You in Grace and Light

Shawn Verrier

Healing stories empowering the individual—Nancy Dudley

March 31, 1992

Dear Rod,
I just got your letter yesterday and was elated to hear the news about Ed. Donna and I have thought of him often, and, of course, we did send him our loving thoughts and Reiki healing. On December 4 we had a particularly intense experience when we were sending Reiki together. We wondered after that if Ed had made the transition to the next world, and have hoped to hear from someone. When I received your letter yesterday I just felt like it was a miracle that Ed has transcended his illness—and it sounds like you experienced much of his journey along with him.
I have thought of you often, wondering what new adventures in healing you were experiencing. I was quite surprised to hear that you have been barred entry into the US. What about Canada? I suppose they have similar policies, which seems so ludicrous. It's not as if you were a drain on either economy!
I am enclosing the first transcript that I have completed. Since I first met you I have been immersed in teaching full-time and counselling part-time (plus some Reiki—I'm enclosing my card). Because of this I have been so busy that I have had a hard time getting to this project to transcribing tapes. I have begun to work on Bozenka's story, but after getting your letter I've decided to interrupt that and begin on Kim's. I will send it to you as soon as I can. The university term is just about over, so I should have some large blocks of time by May to get to this work. You can expect to hear from me about the end of May, or with luck, a bit sooner. I will send things to you as I get them. I know this has been a very long time, but I have tried to attune to the spirit in terms of what is priority as I live each day.
Your idea of a newsletter sounds good; I think sharing people's stories of healing would be particularly meaningful. I have read two books in the past year entitled, <u>Making Miracles</u>—one by Paul C. Roud and one by Paul Pearsall. They were both excellent re: stories of healing. I think that the more people become aware of the possibilities for healing that transcends the kind of cure of symptoms traditional medicine fosters, the more people will begin to choose alternatives. I think the real change will come from the grass roots, not from doctors who are tied to their medical association's definition of good medicine. In other words, I think stories of healing are empowering, and people need to be empowered to explore alternatives.
Best wishes as you continue in your healing work, and I hope you can return to North America—if that is God's plan for you...

God Bless!
Love Nancy

(Calgary, Alberta)

Healing energy research—F.T. H'Doubler

F.T. H'DOUBLER CLINIC, INC.
SUITE 2950 NATIONAL AVENUE MEDICAL BUILDING
1900 SO NATIONAL
SPRINGFIELD, MO 65804

October 10, 1990

TO WHOM IT MAY CONCERN:

RE: Roderick McKenzie Campbell

Roderick McKenzie Campbell has been a close acquaintance of mine for six months. During that time, he has worked in my clinic by using energy healing on complicated patients.   I have been interested in alternative medicine for eighteen years and have served as President of the American Academy of Alternative Medicine in 1985.

I am very hopeful that Mr Campbell will be able to return to the United States and participate in a research project we are now developing where we will measure the energies used most effectively for healing. Presently, we are using micro-energy very successfully in treating arthritis, post-polio syndrome, allergies, etc. I have served several years as Chairman of the Research Committee of Shriner's Hospital, which now have a budget in excess of eighteen million dollars a year. This enables me to have access to people throughout the country with expertise on energy. Mr Campbell would be a prominent member of our research team on this project.

Having personally witnessed favourable results in troublesome patients, I am most enthusiastic in having him return to help in our project.

Sincerely,

F.T. H'Doubler, Jr.,M.D.

FTH'D/ap